TALES AND ANECDOTES COLLECTED

BY THE WPA MONTANA WRITERS' PROJECT

1935–1942

an ORNERY BUNCH

EDITORIAL BOARD
MEGAN HILLER
RICK NEWBY
ELAINE PETERSON
ALEXANDRA SWANEY

TWODOT
HELENA, MONTANA

A · TWODOT · BOOK

2 3 4 5 6 7 8 9 0 MG 04 03 02 01 00

All photos are from the WPA collection, Merrill G. Burlingame Special Collections in the Renne Library at Montana State University, Bozeman. All cover photos by Arthur Rothstein, Farm Security Administration, Montana Writers' Project files.

Library of Congress Cataloging-in-Publication Data
An ornery bunch : tales and anecdotes collected by the WPA Montana
    Writers Project.
        p.   cm.
    ISBN 1-56044-842-3 (softcover)
        1. Montana—Social life and customs Anecdotes.   2. Country life—
Montana Anecdotes.   3. Ranch life—Montana Anecdotes.   4. Montana
Biography Anecdotes.   5. Natural history—Montana Anecdotes.
6. Oral history.   I. Writers' Program of the Work Projects
Administration   in the State of Montana.
F731.6.076   1999
978.6—dc21   99-26427
                                                                         CIP

For extra copies of this book and information about other TwoDot Books, write Falcon, P.O. Box 1718, Helena, Montana 59624; or call 1-800-582-2665. You can also visit our website at www.Falcon.com or contact us by e-mail at falcon@falcon.com.

A portion of the proceeds from the sale of this book will be donated for library development at Montana State University, Bozeman.

CONTENTS

CURIOUS ANIMALS

UNNATURAL TALES

UNDER THE INFLUENCE

TALES OF TRUE WESTERNERS

POKES, PUNCHERS, HERDERS,
THE RANGE, AND THEIR CRITTERS

INTRODUCTION

*I*n the winter of '82–'83, the writer and two brothers (Walter and Ed), together with John S. Barnes and his wife, established a camp in the Snowy Mountains between Buffalo and Rock Creek, and engaged in getting out poles and house logs and shaving shingles for our needs on the homesteads.

We put in the long evenings telling yarns, singing, playing cards, and smoking, of course. We had built our cabin under some big red fir trees in the bottom of a deep canyon. We had a heavy galvanized wire for clothesline running from a corner of the cabin to a big green tree, and it is owing to this fact, no doubt, which caused the phenomena of which I write to occur. I wondered for years how it possibly could transpire, but the great developments along the lines mentioned—radio, wireless, etc.—my readers will no doubt believe me when I state that the weather turning warmer and the frost beginning to thaw out, we were awakened during the night by what at first sounded like a flock of drunken magpies holding a farmers'

convention, but which proved to be a re-hash of our many winter evenings'
songs and stories thawing out.

Source: *Thomas Waddell*
Collector: *B. F. Gordon*

   An Ornery Bunch: Tales and Anecdotes Collected by the WPA Montana Writers' Project was created in an effort to "thaw out" some of the documents collected between 1935 and 1942 by the Federal Writers' Project division of the Works Progress Administration (WPA). An editorial board, including editor Megan Hiller, poet and essayist Rick Newby, Montana State University Associate Professor and Special Collections Librarian Elaine Peterson, and Montana Arts Council Director of Folklife Programs Alexandra Swaney, reviewed a copious collection of tales and anecdotes from the Folklore Studies and the Livestock and Grazing History sections of Montana's WPA archives and chose the most lively, entertaining, complete, and well told stories. The Montana Writers' Project WPA archives offer plenty of intriguing material to choose from, including Chippewa Cree, Gros Ventre, and Blackfeet legends, but the majority of the material in the folklore archives deals with ranching life and lore. We chose to focus this collection on the tales of early pioneers. *An Ornery Bunch* is thus weighted heavily in the direction of cowboys and ranchers, because in addition to culling legends found in the Folklore Studies section, we dipped into the Livestock and Grazing History interviews to find tales.

   We organized our selections based on the focus of the event or the background of the teller. The "Tall Tales" chapter includes those yarns spun out of control. "Curious Animals" includes tales of a pet crow, a talking magpie, highly intelligent horses and dogs, a power-hungry rat, and other notable critters. "Unnatural Tales" describes some of Montana's more unusual natural sights and weather mishaps. The stories in "Under the Influence" remind us of the importance of the saloon in Montana's early towns. "Tales of True Westerners" relates incidents involving well-known western figures such as Liver-eating Johnson, Brother Van, and Theodore Roosevelt. The largest chapter, "Pokes, Punchers, Herders, the Range, and Their Critters," is full of life on Montana's open range. In "Fun with Tenderfoots," we see how Montana's pranksters, including Charles M. Russell, toyed with easterners out west. "Prospectors' Play" is filled with tales of lost mines, still out there for the taking today. The infamous winter of 1886–1887, among other frigid times, is highlighted in "Mother Nature's Winter Wrath." Finally, "Practices, Remedies, and Generally Accepted Lore" reviews some of the old-time practices and beliefs held by early Montana pioneers. Following each selection in this book, we include information about the Writers' Project worker who collected the tale and the source of the tale. In some cases, there is little or no information in the archives about either the recorder or the storyteller. We have sought to preserve the voices of the original tellers in the process of taking what is essentially oral history and presenting it in a readable format. The teller's word choice, grammar, emphasis, and pronunciation are altered as little as possible while still maintaining a readable tale.

Readers will find the truth stretched in all but a few of the yarns, "Tall Tale" or not. As Montana's famous cowboy artist Charlie Russell wrote in *Trails Plowed Under*, "A man in the States might have been a liar in a small way, but when he comes West he soon takes lessons from the prairies, where ranges a hundred miles away seem within touchin' distance, streams run uphill and Nature appears to lie some herself." Nevertheless, Wayndle R. Johnson, one of the collectors working for the Montana Writers' Project, illuminates the value of the "lies" that fill this collection. When Tex Irvine of Belt, Montana, asked whether or not the WPA planned to publish the information it was gathering, Wayndle replied:

Tex, I really don't know just the exact method they use in distributing their publications, but there is one thing that the future generation will have that yours and mine did not have and that is: that when they read the history of America of the past seventy-five years they will be reading facts instead of romantic, though beautiful, tales evolving from the brains of men who wrote history as they wished it rather than the way it actually was.

Tex: Do you believe that all the stories you've heard are any more true than those of the dreamy historians of the past you speak of?

Wayndle: No, I don't. But we must not lose sight of the fact that every representative group of Americans have their own particular style of relating their experiences: like their food they like it well spiced—though it may be sometimes overseasoned, thus destroying the true flavor. I feel sure that America will never lose its sense of humor to the extent that they will censor the tales of Paul Bunyan. After all, Tex, no one accepts Paul's tales as factual, but they are just as American as *Yankee Doodle, Home on the Range,* and *Oh Susanna*—and will be accepted by future generations in the same light.

A WORD ABOUT THE WPA

Unfortunately, much of what Wayndle and other Montana Writers' Project workers collected and wrote would not find its way into the hands of readers for several decades after it was gathered. A U.S. government agency born of President Franklin D. Roosevelt's New Deal administration, the WPA managed to provide gainful employment to many workers who lost their jobs during the Great

Depression. The federal government sponsored labor-intensive projects such as the construction of Montana's Fort Peck Dam—creating jobs that put blue-collar laborers to work. Administrators of the WPA conceptualized the Federal Writers' Project division to offer opportunities to use the skills of white-collar workers who had some writing ability, as well as the polished skills of professional writers. In September of 1935, approximately five months after the WPA was established, the Federal Writers' Project division received final executive approval.

The Federal Writers' Project began with a mission to produce the American Guide series—individual state travel and history guidebooks. The Washington, D.C., headquarters for the project set up state field offices with the direction to gather, compile, and write individual state guides. The guides were to include tourist-based information, most with a positive slant, on the sight-seeing opportunities and history of a state. State field offices submitted final manuscripts to the Federal Writers' Project offices in Washington, D.C., for editing and approval. This approval process proved to be an arduous task for many state offices, including the Montana Writers' Project.

When the Montana Writers' Project completed its contribution to the American Guide series, *Montana: A State Guidebook*, a few other projects followed, including *Copper Camp: The Lusty Story of Butte, Montana, the Richest Hill on Earth*; *Montana: A Profile in Pictures*; *Montanans' Golden Anniversary Humorous History*; and a pamphlet titled "Plants Hardy in Butte." Although the workers for the Montana Writers' Project researched and planned numerous other publications, including a collection of Montana folklore, the Federal Writers' Project was discontinued at the end of 1942 when World War II pulled the U.S. economy out of the Depression. At the close of the Federal Writers' Project, the search began for a suitable home for each state's records. The late Dr. Merrill G.

Burlingame, Montana State University history professor, began negotiating with the Federal Writers' Project to preserve the Montana project's materials at the college in Bozeman. In February 1943, Burlingame received the materials.

Between 1943 and 1995, the Montana's Writers' Project records were available but almost inaccessible to all but the most dedicated researcher due to the lack of organization of the materials. The collection includes more than 250,000 items and occupied 57 linear feet of storage space. In 1995, Montana State University Special Collections Librarian Elaine Peterson applied for and received funding from the Montana Cultural Trust to help reorganize the collection to make it more accessible to all Montanans. We mined the tales and anecdotes in *An Ornery Bunch* from the newly reorganized archives housed in the Merrill G. Burlingame Special Collections in the library at Montana State University.

These are Montana's pioneer tales, spiced just right for the open range of the early West, and, thanks to the efforts of Tex, Wayndle, and other Montana Writers' Project workers and sources, preserved as a part of Montana history.

THE TALES

TALL TALES

*A rancher cleans a cricket trap
in Big Horn County, Montana,
June 1939.*
Farm Security Administration,
photo by Arthur Rothstein (#112)

HORSE RACIN'

*W*e *was havin' one of them horse races in the old days in Billings.* The way they raced then wasn't in a circle. It was between towns and back. They'd set up a spot for a purse and then you could bet on your nag too with anybody you pleased if you had the sheckles to back it up. They's a lot of dirty work goin' on before a race in order that some of the gamblers would have a lead pipe cinch and make a killin' in their bettin', such as cuttin' a horse's mouth or your saddle cinch or something mean and crooked like that.

I had a mighty fine horse then and he had been sired from some good racin' stock from the east. They's one other damned good horse in that race I remember, too, and he was a beautiful black. He's the one I feared would beat me and my pony.

The race was between Billings and Roundup and the purse had

got up to $1,500. You rode over to Roundup, turned around, and high-tailed it back to Billings here, and the first one into Billings won the race. I slept with my horse all the night before the race. I weren't going to take any chances of anybody crookin' my horse.

We got started the next day, seventeen of us, all fair and square. I knowed the lay of the land between here and Roundup like a book. I'd been over it time and again. I wore moccasins fer a special purpose. Being a young critter then, I could run like a flash myself and had outrun many horses just to see what I could do.

Well, in this certain race I got way ahead of the rest of 'em right off the bat and when we come to a stretch of country that was nude of cactus, I'd leap off and run alongside of my horse. You see I's playing smart and was savin' my horse fer that final stretch. Most of the rest of 'em caught up with me at Roundup but their horses were showin' the strain more 'n mine was. Mine was as fresh as a daisy. Of course my own withers was lathered up some and I was a-wheezin' fer breath 'cause I'd run nigh onto fifteen miles.

That black was a comin' right along as I feared. When we's about twelve miles from Billings I give my horse the nudge and we left that black in our dust. Well, that black kept crowdin' right up again and again and I knowed my pony had a lot of reserve yet. When we was within sight of Billings that dad-ratted black scalywag was right alongside of us again. It didn't look so good so I leaped back off my horse and ran 'er a-foot fer a spell until me and my pony were a good five hundred yards in the lead. Then I leaped back on my pony and give the horse hell the rest of the way in. By God that black moved right up and was a crowdin' me so that I thought I'd have to get off and run myself a-foot to get ahead. If there'da been another hundred yards I might have lost. That sure was some black pony.

I was pretty mad at my pony fer comin' so close to gettin' beat. So I raced my nag to Huntley where I had a ranch then. Ever so often I'd set down on a boulder to rest and wait fer my pony to catch up and he'd be so damned mad. When he'd get near the boulder I'd be sittin' on, his ears were laid back flat to his head and his teeth were all out ready to take a hunk out of my leg, but I'd scamper on and get out of his reach. I sure burnt him up and it serves him right because he danged near lost that race for me.

Source: William E. "Billy the Kid" Huntington of Lockwood, Montana. At the time of this interview, Mr. Huntington was seventy-nine years old and had lived in Montana for sixty-five years.
Collector: Chet M. Simpson

RATTLESNAKE JOE

*R*attlesnake Joe was an odd duck. He had no use fer the wimmen and furthermore, he's in cahoots with the devil. That's how come he aks like he done.

Everybody always give Snakey Joe, that's what he was knowed as, wagon room when he come ter town. Billings was nuthin' but a bunch of saloons 'n shacks, 'n the streets were mud or dust depending on the weather, and they were lined with hitch-racks up and down. Joe lived somewhere in the dry land country between the Yellowstone and the Musselshell. He was of average height, bald as a cue ball on a frosty morning, and the lightest and scarcest beard ye ever seed. He had a thin hatchet face with about two teeth in his upper jaw; fangs as people dubbed them. It was said if Joe ever bit ya with them there fangs ye'd be pizened fer shore and die on the spot. But I believe Joe wasn't that bad as he's painted.

Snakey Joe was an old gent when I knowed him and he was doing nuthin' but peddlin' snake oil in old whiskey bottles to them that wanted it. Them that used it sed it was good fer the roomatiz, lumbago, and sitch like. When he sold all he put up he'd spend hours gettin' soused to the gills in the saloons. He always drank alone and nobody cared to have truck with him 'cept mebby Whiskey Smith.

Whiskey Smith was a black-bearded, barrel-bodied, bullying gent of no-count reputation who carried two guns 'n was always on the prod to use them. He killed fer the love of killin' and no livin' skunk ever had a broader yaller road down his spinal column than Whiskey Smith. Bout the only recommendin' thing of old Whiskey was that he always bought the best rawhide boots in the West and kept 'em shinin' like a greased nigger's heel. The shortest course to a wooden overcoat in them days was to walk over and spit on them glistenin' boots. You shore wuz headed fer hell from then on.

Well this here Whiskey wuz never missin' a chance ter insult poor Snakey Joe. He'd say, "Here cums thet cre-chure lower'n a snake's belly." All kinds of dirty remarks he'd say. One I knowed must of angered Snakey Joe wuz, "They tell me Joe was suckled by a bitch rattler." Joe'd jist keep on drinkin' his special brand of liquid pisen and never give him no heed. The snake oil peddler never wore a gun fer protection and fer this reason Whiskey couldn't kill him unless he had a damned good excuse in front of all of the boys. I knowed these two was going to come to no good end.

Anyway I wuz going to tell ya 'bout his snake ranch. I bin out there a number of times and I never finds Joe very sociable and very anxious to show ya around. I talks to him quite confidential like and brags his snake oil up to the skies. I sez how I allows it keeps thet danged roomatiz out of my right knee and chases it over in my left foot and corners it there and then skiddooes it out my big toes and I'm rid of the pesky stuff. You know I guess he'd bin so long without kind words thet he actually grins and acts happy.

"Shore," he sez. "Come on 'n I'll show ya around." So I goes on a toor.

Son, I will never see so many pizen, wrigglin' creatures before or since. They is crazy as hungry chickens to see Snakey Joe come near the pens. The slimy devils crowd the fences and lap out their tongues like a pantin' dog. He shows me his pride and joy which is little fellers jist out of the shell. Then he gets to a pen of bigger youngsters which he shows me are cuttin' their teeth. He picks up a youngster that has cut his first tooth and opens its mouth as proud as a new papa. He teases the rascal and the pint-sized reptile coils up and wags a stubby tail with a red pimple on it. It all is a laugh 'cept that the little devil strikes and bites Snakey Joe. Joe puts him back in the pen and I see the spot bitten raise into a blister. Joe shrugs his shoulder and sez, "Just like the hives, it'll go away."

I've got about enough curiosity satisfied and I hankers to leave fer I fear I'll dream about snakes. "Ya ain't seen nuthin' yet," he sez and takes me to a special pen. Here is three big females he sez; all fat and lazy. One is a yaller rattler and the other two are diamondbacks. There ain't one of 'em with less than ten rattles on 'em. They grows angry at my appearance and sets up a din that sounds like three baby rattles cut loose at once and they is all coiled ready to strike.

The rattlesnake stench is so strong it about gags me. I watch Joe's play for I'm not hankerin' to stick around much longer. Joe opens the gate and boldly walks into the pen with them varmints and locks the gate after him. He calls the yaller one Violet and the other two he had names fer too but I don't catch them 'cause I'm watchin' Joe get snapped at by Violet. Violet calms down and when she quits rattlin', the other two shet up too. He talks so sentimental to yaller back thet I think mebby I should turn my back and let them be alone. I gather Violet is an unforgetable name in Joe's past.

No doubt it is the name of the two-legged female snake thet did Joe wrong. I figure it is Joe's subtle way of revenge by naming a yaller snake after her. Then Snakey Joe hollers, "Ya wanta see my snake orchestra?"

Well, I've seen about everything and I sez, "Yeh, Joe, go ahead." So he walks over to the fence wall and takes off a mouth harp I hain't noticed at all. Then he fetches down three tiny tinklin bells and the snakes stick up their rattle-tipped tails. He attaches these tiny bells of different tones and so help me Hannah as I live and breathe I'll never hear and see a sight like thet. He cups his hands over his mouth harp and plays "Little Pal" and these female rattlers playing accompaniment with the bells and swaying their bodies above their coils. Then to top it all off another big rattler crawls out of a hole, wraps his tail around a drum stick and starts beatin' on a big rawhide drum that I didn't see sittin' in the corner of the pen.

Snakey Joe had a rotten deal with Fate when it came time fer Joe ta leave these grounds. It was Whiskey Smith that done it as you have guessed. He trumped up some flimsy excuse and perforated Joe's torso with his sixguns in one of the saloons. Whiskey Smith stood over his victim's body and gloated about his cowardly deed. But Joe was avenged. Violet, the yaller rattler, crawled out from dead Joe's sleeve and bit Whiskey Smith through those bootiful boots. Smith shot the rattler 'n died later but cried like a baby. Nobody expected old Rattlesnake Joe to have thet snake up his sleeve but it served Whiskey Smith his just desserts.

Source: William E. "Billy the Kid" Huntington of Lockwood, Montana. At the time of this interview, Mr. Huntington was seventy-nine years old and had lived in Montana for sixty-five years.
Collector: Chet M. Simpson
Collector's Note: After telling the above story, Mr. Huntington further related that the curse of Rattlesnake Joe remained. The swamper in this saloon stole the highly polished boots off the dead body of Whiskey Smith. Two days later the saloon swamper

was found dead in his cabin. A renegade cowpoke took possession of the eye-catching boots and dropped dead on Main Street with the boots only on for about two hours. The undertaker who was getting so much business all of a sudden, not knowing he was hurting his trade, investigated the boots and found a big rattlesnake fang still stuck in the leather. The boots hung in the undertaker's parlor as a symbol of death and nobody would take them as a gift even knowing the fang was extracted.

Extra Big Grasshoppers

One year I and a young sprout I had working for me were hightailin' our ponies up the Yellowstone valley about where Custer is now. I had to get some race horses in Billings and then make the trip back. This young sprout had a gunnysack of chewing tobacco strapped to the back of his saddle and I had the grub for both of us strapped to the back of my saddle.

The country we were traveling through was barren as a bone—hardly any vegetation of any kind at all. Even the soap weeds had been eaten to the ground. You couldn't see a living thing. I knowed something was wrong. I seed "road apples" every now and then; and they weren't from a horse or cow or moose or anything I'd ever seed before. The kid that was with me sez, "What the devil cleaned everything up like this?" I shook my head not knowing myself. Our horses were gettin' skittish and snortin' their dissatisfaction.

Well sir, we come upon the critters that was doing all the land stripping. They were the biggest gall-durned grasshoppers I seed in my time. They had big purple eyes and dirty brown bodies and no wings to speak of. The two we chanced upon were standing guard at a couple of prairie dog holes. A prairie dog came out while we were sittin' on our horses with our mouths open. This one grasshopper leaped like a cat and pounced on the prairie dog. The dog squealed and kicked but it did no good. The 'hopper ate him on the spot. These grasshopper critters were meat eaters, too.

I was for getting out of there as quick as possible and I told my partner so at the time. We rode on a little farther and found seven or eight 'hoppers sittin' around with big bellies. I soon seed what they had eaten. It was a yearlin' calf. There was nothing left but the carcass. The 'hoppers were pickin' their teeth with the ribs of the calf carcass. It seems that calf was a bull calf and was a little tough and they had to pick some of the meat out of their teeth.

My partner was signaling me to get going. We started to whip up our horses and dash out of this barren country. I noticed that the gunnysack of chewing tobacco was gone. In our excitement we lost it. Well, we had to have our chewing tobacco if we never had anything else. I'd druther we lost the grub sack instead of the tobaccy. Upon the discovery we immediately back-tracked our trail.

We hunted and tracked and ran into more of these purple-eyed grasshoppers. Some of 'em were ferocious at being spied on and being disturbed and would kick at us with those big hind feet. Finally we came upon the sack of tobaccy. It hardly could be seen for the crowd of critters wallowing over it.

The grasshoppers had torn the gunnysack open and were chewing our tobacco. As we rode up all we could hear was, "Spitooey. Spitooey." They were spitting all over the landscape. First one would let fly and then another. All of this energetic expectoration was raising such a ruckus that our horses were rearing and rantin' and wantin' to get out of there.

Well, I'm tellin' you those grasshoppers had forgotten one thing. All that spittin' of theirs would eventually lead to one thing, a big drink of water. There wasn't any water only that was twenty-five miles away at the river. They stampeded to the river in large herds, killing a number in the rush. It was mighty hot that day and the majority of the 'hoppers died of thirst and what did get to the river floundered. Yes sir, we killed 'em all on chewing tobaccy and it served the fools right.

Source: William E. "Billy the Kid" Huntington of Lockwood, Montana. At the time of this interview, Mr. Huntington was seventy-nine years old and had lived in Montana for sixty-five years.
Collector: Chet M. Simpson

MONTANA FERTILE SOIL

*Y*ou won't believe me but this is the Gospel truth. They talk about how good and fertile the soil is in other states of the union. I'm tellin' you that Montana has some damned good soil.

You take the soil there on Poverty Flats. We never knew what could be growed on it for years. We were so busy grazing cattle, gettin' 'em to the market, and countin' our money after it was all over with.

Things changed and it became apparent that good money could be made in raising wheat and other crops. The story I'm arrivin' at is about vegetables that could be raised. This here Poverty Flats had the most wonderful soil for gardens I ever saw in my life. It was jet black soil and it seemed to have life in it when you'd pick a hunk of it up and squeeze it in the palm of your hand. Sometimes it'd remind you of overbaked Devil's Food Cake. There is no soil in Iowa or Minnesota that could beat it.

The first year I planted a garden I'll never forget. I had took special care in selectin' this spot near the river and when I plowed and harrowed it it seemed to be rarin' to get that seed in its vitals so it could show what could be done.

I took my seed out one nice sunshiny day and when I got set to plant I noticed that the only garden seed I had was pickles. Somehow I had lost the other garden seed on the way to the garden patch. I went ahead and sowed my pickle seed and when I got a quarter of the patch sowed I turned around and thought I'd blew my work. To my surprise the bloomin' seed was sprouted through the soil already. As I stood there in awe and my mouth wide open, I saw little specks of yellow formin' on the vines. They were pickle flowers. In another minute the vines began to fork out in all directions all over the garden patch.

I got scared and started to run toward the ranch house which was a mile away. I could hear them vines growing across the prairie and makin' a noise that resembled the wind a-blowin' through cattails. I put on more speed and ran as fast as I could but those vines were gainin' on me. Pretty soon I came slap-bang up against a pink-yellow barrier and here were carrots as big as fence posts that had split the ground wide open and were growin' above the soil. They were the seed I had dropped on the way to the garden patch and the seed I had spilled out on the ground.

Well, these pickle vines came growing on by me and when I did find my way around the carrot barrier I had to go through these vines. Pickles were forming on them already. I worked my way with some difficulty through shoulder high vines and bruised my shoulders on many a pickle before I got to the house.

When I arrived at the house I breathed a sigh of relief but I was scared stiff because these vines were growin' right over the ranch house and I didn't know how I was goin' to stop 'em. I reached into my hip pocket to get my Climax and I had to pick out a couple of pickles before I could get to my chawin' tobacco. I got my cud all moistened up and was goin' into the house to rest up a bit and think things out. When I opened the door it knocked a ripe cucumber as big as a melon off a vine and it came down and hit me a whack on the head nearly knocking me out.

Boy! I'm tellin' you that Montana soil is really fertile and when them vines quit growin', we had enough pickles to supply the whole United States that year. That just goes to show you how good Montana soil is.

Source: E. L. "Dick" Grewell of Billings, Montana. At the time of this interview, Mr. Grewell was seventy-one years old, a retired rancher, and had lived in Montana for fifty-two years.
Collector: Chet M. Simpson

RIDIN' A JACKRABBIT

I noticed one year a herd of deer grazing on the hills nearby Poverty *Flats and something unusual I noticed was one of the deer kept sittin' down on its hind haunches.* No deer does that but before I could see anymore of that certain doe, the deer scared and disappeared in a gully.

I didn't hear nor see anymore of that unusual doe until one of the cowboys I had workin' for me says he sure as hell saw the biggest damned jackrabbit a-runnin' with a herd of deer. He says to me that it was fully as big as the deer it was keeping company with. I told him I allowed he had been drinkin' some powerful Panther Poison, whiskey to you, to see anything like that. But he said he'd be willin' to swear up and down on a stack of bibles that it was the Gospel truth. The upstart of it was that I had a glimpse of the same thing myself and I know I was cold sober.

The talk got worse. More fellers saw that same big jack runnin' wild with them deer. Finally, I guess, everybody's imagination got the better of 'em and they were for goin' and ropin' or runnin' that big jack into the corral. You see what was comin' up was that some of the fellers had a idea in the back of their heads to throw a saddle on that overgrown jackrabbit. They's been braggin' amongst themselves how good a bronco buster they were.

Well, the sum and essence of it all was that they did get the jack cut out of the herd of deer. There were more riders than deer and jackrabbit put together. They ought to but they couldn't lay a rope on him because he was as shifty as all get out.

They got him in the corral and right away he commenced to get lonesome for them deer. He no more commenced than he decided to leap out of the corral, which he did quicker than the time it takes to wink your eye. The boys went right after him and, with three relays of horses, they managed to keep the big jackrabbit on Poverty Flats and to run the poor devil ragged. They run him so long and so often that his tongue hung out a yard and being a resourceful critter just slung his tongue over his shoulder and went on.

When the boys headed him toward the corral this time, he was mighty glad to stop there for a rest. They got him in the chute and throwed a saddle on him. The biggest braggert got on and away the rabbit and rider went. The jackrabbit took about three crow hops to kinda adjust himself to the additional weight and to do a little calculatin'.

From then on I couldn't tell no more what happened than the man in the moon. It just happened so furious and so fast that it couldn't be recorded or seen by the naked eye. As good as I could see the jack started with a stiff, snappy, neck-snappin' jolt and the cowboy's hat went spinnin' away up in the air. Then before you knew it, you saw the cowpuncher shoot up clear of the jack and right through the center of that spinnin' hat as though it was made of paper. I never saw anything like it. The puncher was shot up so far that when he lit, it damned near killed him.

The jack went tearin' across the flats and up a coulee with that saddle and halter on. We saw him days later and he'd got rid of the halter but the saddle was still with him. The saddle had flopped over and was under his withers. He wore that saddle that way for months and it was the cause of makin' him jump like that when he'd run. You know, to this day all the jackrabbits of Poverty Flats run the same way as though they had a saddle hung counter-wise under their withers. Well, it is needless to say that none of the boys ever turned a hair to re-saddle that buckin' jackrabbit and it's the truth, so help me.

Source: E. L. "Dick" Grewell of Billings, Montana. At the time of this interview, Mr. Grewell was seventy-one years old and had lived in Montana for fifty-two years. Collector: Chet M. Simpson

Ride the Pinto Trout, Cowboy

I shouldn't have done it, going into the mountains on that solo fishing trip.

I was hired out as a bronco buster and had been working hard all summer. I asked the boss to let me have one or two weeks off in the mountains taking 'er easy; besides I had been recently throwed from a mean bronc and I had a broken rib. Then my kidneys and liver must have swapped places because my guts didn't feel any too good inside.

The boss was a good egg and not only gave me permission to go but consented to lend me a pack horse and all the trimmings including camping equipment and grub. I took along what fishing tackle I had which wasn't much more than a good line and about three hooks. I was headed for a lake the boys were eternally telling me to go to and try my luck. They said there were some mighty big fish in that mountain lake.

I arrived at the lake after a tough climb for myself and the horses. The horses were hard to handle especially since they hadn't been used to mountain travel. And when their nostrils would get a sniff of a wildcat or puma, those cats sure put the fear in them ponies.

After arriving at the shore of the lake, I set up camp and looked around for a good willow to use as a fishing pole. I easily found what I wanted and cut it and trimmed it down for use in the morning. I also made a crude type of canoe for use the next morning since the fellows said the only way to get them big ones was to get a boat and paddle out into the center of the lake.

The next morning I arrived and it seemed that I couldn't wait and I got up out of the blankets around 4 A.M. There was another reason that caused me to get aroused that early. It was so damned cold up on that mountain and I wasn't used to it, being used to the valley climate. I cooked my breakfast and then to try out my pole and line I cast a couple of times in the shore water of the lake and caught two three-pound trout. I didn't really want to catch such big ones right away. I wanted to use my first catch as bait but if these three-pounders were all the smaller they had, well it was all right with me.

I put my equipment in the canoe and paddled out to the center of the lake. A sly grin was on my face for I could see myself in the reflection of the lake water. I couldn't keep back my elation. I had a large hook and to this I strung one of the three-pounders I had caught. The three-pounder wasn't dead yet and he kinda come to life again. He swam around in a half-dazed manner. This was all the better to lure the big uns.

The sun was pretty well up on its climb in the sky and I hadn't got a nibble. I was cussing my idea of using a canoe. What you should have is a flat-bottomed boat. Then the three-pounder was getting so lively that it seemed I was fishing all over again for him. All of a sudden something took my bait with such force that my arms were nearly pulled out of their sockets. I had a death grip on the willow pole. It was a good thing. Before I could realize what was going on, I and the canoe were being towed.

Well, to make a long story short I was towed around that lake for two hours or more and every chance I got I'd wind the slack line around my pole. I got the big fellow alongside the canoe and he was fully as long as my canoe and a pinto in his markings. My God he was big fish. He kept pulling alongside of the canoe and every time I'd try to rein him into the shore, he'd circle the lake again.

Finally I got desperate. I had my boots and spurs on. The canoe was getting slopped with water and would sink if I didn't do something and quick. Why not straddle his back and ride him into shore? The thought no more occurred to me than I leaped on his back and put the spurs to him.

He went wild then. We circled that lake as though it was a puddle and him a bucking all the way. I was soaked to the hide with lake water. I got another good hold on the willow pole and pulled the line tight causing his head to clear the water and then I headed him ashore right for my camp. It was a straight away and we musta made sixty knots an hour. I never traveled so fast in all my life and I thought the wind would tear the ears off of my head.

We were headed for a wide sandy beach and I didn't know how we were going to stop going at that speed. Well, we skidded for twenty-five yards across that sandy beach and the friction from the sand fried that big trout and burnt the seat out of my pants. I jumped off just in time or I'd have been fried and if you don't believe it I've got the burnt pants to prove it.

Source: Charles B. "Charlie" Simmons of Billings, Montana. At the time of this interview, Mr. Simmons, an old-time bronc buster, was seventy-four years old and had lived in Montana for most of his life.
Collector: Chet M. Simpson
Collector's Note: I didn't ask him to produce the burnt pants.

SWAMP RABBIT

I had the oddest pet when I was batching near Joliet, Montana, 'long
Rock Creek. He was half jackrabbit and half something else.

When I was single I thought I'd raise a few milk cows and some
wheat along the flats near Rock Creek below Joliet. I had a nice log
cabin of my own, a barn, and stables. My shepherd dog got kicked
in the head by a colt and died so I had made up my mind if I should
go to town again I would get another dog.

I was hunting wild turkeys in the swamp land near the river
when I heard a lot of squealing. I thought perhaps a snake had
caught a bird. Nearing the point of disturbance, I came into a
clearing under some big trees. There lay a young rabbit, with the
biggest head, a-kickin' his big boney hind feet and squealing like
he was hurt.

I picked him up and petted him and he still let out some hideous squeals. He was part jackrabbit, that was certain, but what
other breed he had in him I could never tell. I petted him for awhile
and he quieted down and then I took him home. Well, sir, I kept
him and raised him and he became about as big as a dog. S'fact.

He had all the dogs and cats in the vicinity buffaloed. Whenever any stray dog came near him and barking and growling, he'd
never move an inch. Just sit there. As soon as the dog came close
enough he'd reach out with a hind foot and bop mister dog on the
nose. He had educated hind feet. I say that because he could do
remarkable things with them. He could talk to any rabbit in the
swamp by rapping out certain rabbit conversation by thumping the
ground with his big hind feet. He'd call all his girl friends up this
way and arrange a date. S'fact because in the spring there was
much ground beating going on and then he'd disappear for days.

The next winter when we were sitting around the fires and not
doing anything, I hit upon the idea of teaching Dummie the Morse

code. I called him Dummie from the first day I found him. He turned out, however, to be a lot smarter than at first appeared.

I had two apple boxes empty and laying around the cabin. I hit upon the idea of rapping out the Morse code on one box while he sat on the other and learned it.

Well, sir, before winter was up he could send or receive any message. He was that good. Dummie was of great value on the hunt. He could leisurely come into a flock of wild turkeys, or grouse, or ducks, then slip over to the nearest hollow log and send me the latitude and longitude. It really spoiled the sport of the thing. It was too easy.

Woodpeckers were Dummie's downfall. I told him and told him that woodpeckers never sent code messages. He was never sure. Always he thought they were talking to him. I tried and tried to explain that woodpeckers did rapping to drill holes into the wood to bury worms. He never thoroughly understood it, I guess.

Anyway one day we were hot on the trail of some fat wild turkeys. Dummie telegraphed to me from the nearest hollow log. "Latitude 30, Longitude 24. Three big gobblers. That is all."

A red-headed woodpecker intercepted the message and rapped back before I could get to the nearest stump. "Go to hell. That is all." I always thought that woodpecker was a lot smarter than he pretended. Well, sir, Dummie was a bunny of tender feelings and that did it. He thought I sent the message and make joke with him. He disappeared from the premises entirely. I've looked and hunted high and low but I've never found out what became of him to this day.

Source: Ralph L. Simpson of Billings, Montana. At the time of this interview, Mr. Simpson was sixty-five years old. He was an old-time rancher whose ranch was once located on Cold Creek of Shane Ridge between what is now known as Columbus and Joliet, Montana.
Collector: Chet M. Simpson

Tame Deer

*I*t *was after the homesteaders had taken over this country and the old-time cowman was almost an extinct human.* About the only thing I could get fer work that certain winter was a pittlin's job of milking cows. I'd always regarded that kind of endeavor as degrading and not a job fer a cowpuncher. You had to come down off your high horse then 'cause things were changing fast—as much as you might hate it.

This cow milkin' spread was near the mountains and the critters would parade up and down the small valleys near the barns. My rhoomatiz was a-botherin' me so much I knew they's a whale of a storm coming pretty quick. Sure enough it busted loose on us from the north and it was a doozy. It snowed considerable and then blew the snow all over creation. Cattle were lost.

We had plenty of feed fer these milkers and just kept them in the barn and no critter was hurt none. Week after week this cold spell went on and the temperature dropped to thirty below zero. Pretty soon we began to see flocks of deer comin' out of the hills and mountains lookin' fer feed. They's starved and practically all their grazing was covered with deep snow.

I didn't pay much attention to them deer hangin' around the barn and when finishing up milkin' one night I noticed I felt unusually tired. I looked over the bunch I'd milked and I seed I'd milked two does and never knowed it. Them deer were so starved that gentleness come natural. They had sidled up alongside the cow critters and I hadn't noticed it fer they were eatin' out of the mangers. We were gettin' that deer milk besides the cow milk.

The deer milk got the boys awful springy on their feet and they played leapfrog standin' straight up and not bendin' a-back carryin' their milk pails and milk stools all the same time. A fence or eight foot corral wasn't no obstacle 'cause all it took was a light fantastic and you were over it. After a little practice I got so I could leap to the top of the haystack and save the trouble of climbing the ladder. Boy! That deer milk would sure make ya light on your tootsies. A jackrabbit kept hangin' around eatin' off the haystack and I got mad at him one day and tore out after him to give him a good scare. I guess I musta overdid myself because before I knowed it I run clean on past him fer a hundred yards before I could stop myself. The jackrabbit came along runnin' fer dear life and thinkin' I was still behind him. I just retched out and grabbed him by those big ears. He was so skeered and surprized that he died from heart failure on the spot. I was a little surprised myself concerning my speed.

Well, I was a little leery of this diet of deer milk and one day while shovelin' hay out of the mow I bumped my head on a rafter. There was quite a lump on my head and it wouldn't go away. Pretty soon another lump formed itself on the other side of my head in exactly the same spot. I couldn't figure it out and neither one of the lumps was sore anymore. The boys said, "Bill, you're sure growin' horns fer being Old Prong Tail hisself and fer being so ornery. You better look and see if ya ain't sproutin' a forked tail." I was skeered as all get out and I knowed it was that deer milk. I laid off that stuff and even quit chewin' terbacco 'cause it resembled a cud and would have some influence. Yep, the lumps went away, finally. I musta been destined fer antlers and if it hadn't a been fer my quick thinkin' I'da ketched myself in a fine mess if I'da drank another drop of that deer milk.

Source: William E. "Billy the Kid" Huntington of Lockwood, Montana. At the time of this interview, Mr. Huntington was seventy-nine years old and had lived in Montana for sixty-five years.
Collector: Chet M. Simpson

BUCKY, THE BIGGEST LIAR
IN MONTANA TERRITORY

*B*ucky *was one of those cowboys.* He ran 30 Mile Ranch and was reputedly the biggest liar in Montana territory, although many others unsuccessfully boasted of that distinction. One day Bucky was riding range many miles from any humans, when his horse chanced to stumble into a prairie dog hole and fell, pinning Bucky securely underneath. For a time he lay there gazing up into a blazing sky not conscious of any suffering until the first numbness wore off and then acute sickening pains began to shoot through him and Bucky knew that his leg was broken. He tried grimly to wriggle free of the dead weight of his horse but every cautious movement sent agonizing stabs of pain through him. He was in a serious predicament. He shouted, doubtless cursed energetically, smoked and shouted, cursed and waited, anxious eyes searching the plains for a passing rider. Night fell and a chill wind crept over the silent prairie and still no one came to the rescue. By this time Bucky had reached this dramatic moment in the story and he had thoroughly impressed his listeners with the gravity of the situation. One of them who should have known better broke out, "What did you do Bucky?"

"Me?" answered Bucky. "Why I finally had to walk eight miles to find a pole with which to pry that darned hoss off my leg."

Source: *Glendolin Damon Wagner originally wrote this piece for* The Roundup Record Tribune *on December 5, 1935.*
Collector: *Evelyn M. Rhoden*

THIS ONE GOT AWAY

A number of years ago, a couple of old timers got together. In the course of the evening they got to spinning yarns. Old Pete Brandaway, after taking a few too many of the little glasses our genial host "Buzz" Bradford set before him, finally broke out into one of his "truth-splitting escapades."

Yuh don't need to believe it. I don't expect yuh to, but it's true. I'll swear to God on a stack of bibles if it ain't. It happened in 1896, I believe. Old Man Hoggins—he's dead now—and me was busy on a ranch by the Yallerstone gittin' busy for the fall roundup. We had a coupla mules on that place that we sorta had it in fer. Didn't like mules in them days any more'n now. But anyway, one day she was rainin' cats and fiddlesticks. Damn, but that was some rain! It started in the mornin' around 2 o'clock and lasted for a good whole week. Durin' that time the old Yallerstone rose higher's higher until she begins runnin' over her banks. And the water was muddy, you know what I mean, riley, yaller, boilin' muddy. That's how she gets her name.

Well, at the end of that week the rain stops and the sun comes out a-scorchin' for all she's worth. A week later, after the river goes down a bit, I says to Clem, "Clem," says I, "Let's go fishin'! There's nothin' like a good fat catfish fried nice and brown, with plenty of flour and salt and pepper."

"Darned if it hain't," says he and off we goes.

Now, in them days there warn't any of this law business. Anybody that had a line used it, sinkers and all. We fixed up a good stout piece of cord and throws her out, baited with a coupla hunks of beef into a likable hole, deep and quiet-like. After that we waits until mornin', then goes back. When we arrive we was floored. The little bush we'd tied the cord to was uprooted and gone. There wasn't a sight of the line.

Old Clem looks her over and says, solemn-like, "That hain't no fish done that, Pete. No sir. Some old log musta got caught in that line."

I shook my head, not knowin' what to think and set about fixin' another line. This time I got some new bailin' wire and fixed up some hooks, baited 'em and threw 'em out. I tied that line to a young cottonwood and went back to bed. The next day Clem'n I walked out to look at our line. It was there but the young cotton-wood looked plenty sick, as though it'd taken a beatin' by some big wind. All around in the mud wuz marks where it'd been lashed against the ground. After lookin' matters over I grabs hold of the wire and begins pullin' it careful like. Pretty soon we had it on shore. About four feet from the end it had been bitten off slick as a whistle. Was BITTEN OFF!

[Collector's Note: The speaker, Brandaway, paused a moment to glare drunkenly at an intruder who had laughed at him. The fellow squelched, he resumed.]

There wuz teeth marks all over that there wire. It'd been chewed, bitten—I tell yuh, like as though some one'd gone at it with a pair of pliers. That settled it. I worked most all that mornin' on a new line. When I came outa the blacksmith shop I had a steel moorin' nothin' could bite through. An' hooks to go with it, one hundred feet of wire'n steel. Well, right after dinner, amongst the jeers of the boys and the boss, I went down to the river draggin' Clem along. He seemed sorta wantin' to hang back, but he came along after I'd convinced him it wasn't no joke the boys'd been layin' on us. I had a hunch and I was goin' to play that hunch!

The boss laughingly had two of the boys hitch up them two mules I told you about and had a pair of double trees and a chain to attach to the line I'd fixed up. Well, I tossed out that there line for the third time. We'd waited quite a spell when the little cotton-wood I'd tied her to began to quiver, just a little bit. Then the line gives a yank and the tree goes flat down on her face. Yuh oughta seen the boys stare. Then it flopped back up, lookin' kinda scared like. There was a few minutes pause and then it goes down again. This time the roots make a suckin' sound.

"Hi Clem!" I yells, "Bring over them mules and be spat about it."

Clem brought 'em over and I attached the chain to the double trees. Then, durin' one of the lulls in the tuggin's on that line, I unslips the noose on the tree and gives it over to the mules.

"Start 'em slow," I says, anticipatin' the pull. The words had no sooner left my lips when it comes. Clem yells at the mules and they digs in. Their fetlocks looks like steel stakes driven in the mud.

"Keep pullin'!" I yells. Then there's a lull and the slack comes in. Clem takes advantage and lams the mules up the bank ten feet when the second yank comes, settlin' them two mules right down on their sandy butts and upsettin' Clem. The boys on the bank yells.

"Hold 'er Clem!"

Well, we keeps that up. Seven times the line yanks and seven times we gains ground. On the seventh lull when Clem clucks to the old mules we looks real sharp. Suddenly outa that yaller, muddy water there pokes the horriblest, ugliest head I never seen. A catfish it was. And boy! What a monster! Ten feet across that flat, gray head of his. I could see its old feelers wavin' in the air, willow-like.

The boys yell again and then somethin' happens I never hope to see again. That old cat lifts up a tail like the broad side of a hill and slams her into the water with a mighty ker-splash. Then it yanks its head and starts headin' for the deep.

Clem yells, caught unawares. I yell. The boys yell, but before we'd got the words outta our mouths the fish was gone, and with it, the line, the single trees and the mules. Clem was knocked over backward in the rush. I tell yuh it was appallin! Them mules screamin' in sheer terror, was shipped into the water quicker'n a wink. For a few seconds the old river boiled. A regular geyser shot up, coverin' us all over with muddy Yallerstone. Then it was I caught another glimpse of the big flat head, bigger'n a barn with a mule strugglin' in its mouth and that was all. Two minutes later there wasn't a trace of nothin'. All there was was a gouged out track in the mud where the two mules and the line had slashed past.

Source: Pete Brandaway
Collector: Keith Dickman of Missoula, Montana
Collector's Note: There wasn't anything said after that yarn. We simply got up and left without a word. I had copy to write for the next day's column in the Gazette *and Pete—well, I think he went to bed. What else could he do?*

A VERY NARROW ESCAPE

*D*uring the summer, the story is often told of the camper up in the hills who went in swimming. That year being an unusually wet year the mosquitoes had grown to an abnormally large size, many of them being about the size of hawks, with long spiked bills.

As the camper emerged from the stream a large flock of the hungry mosquitoes swooped down upon him. The unlucky camper looked wildly about him for some protection from the hungry horde and seeing a large iron kettle near the camp fire he turned it upside down and crawled under it. He was kneeling there in the darkness under the big iron kettle hoping against hope that the mosquitoes would soon forget all about him, when suddenly he felt something poke him in the back. He looked up and saw to his dismay that the mosquitoes were drilling through the iron kettle to get at him. In desperation he picked up a rock that happened to be lying under the kettle and began clinching the stingers as fast as each mosquito would drill through the kettle. Finally just as the last mosquito was firmly clinched to the kettle the swarm flew away with the kettle leaving the camper with no proof of his very narrow escape.

Source: Elmer Baird of Roundup, Montana

Duck Hunting

*D*ucks . . . *say, mebby I ain't a duck hunter.* But you know, I don't have time to take care of 'em after I've shot 'em, anyway, not right away. An' that makes things bad, because you know what happens in them-there circumstances.

Wall, that was a problem botherin' me for a long time. It bothered me plumb awful until one night I set me down an' figured out a way to save them ducks after I shot 'em. When I go huntin' now, I jest doctor up my shells by packin' salt in among the birdshot. So when I shoot one of them ducks, the salt keeps it fresh until I find time to cook 'em!

Source: Tex Ireland of Cut Bank, Montana, was known as a guide, cowboy and professional rodeo rider.
Collector: Ralph C. Henry of Missoula, Montana

CURIOUS ANIMALS

"Steer Montana," the world's largest steer, was exhibited in thirty-nine states. "Steer Montana" was 6 feet tall with a 9-foot, 2-inch girth, and weighed 3,980 pounds.

Credit: (#601)

CURIOUS ANIMALS

HAWK-CLAW JIM AND A CROW NAMED JOE

I worked for a lot of outfits in my time and had a cow spread of my own once. But I worked for a spread here in Montana that had the oddest duck I ever met up with.

I palled around with him for a while. His name was Hawk-claw Jim. I wouldn't know what his last name was and I guess he didn't care to have anybody get too inquisitive. He didn't hanker me as a pal much and had a desire to be a lone wolf. He had killed somebody in Texas and had to get out in a hurry.

He was about the most superstitious *hombre* I ever ran across. Well, in those days no puncher was entirely free from some form of "Indian belief." They used to make fun of the Indians making medicine and carrying a medicine bag, but I've always found that there was a lot of whites that were more so on the fearing angle.

Hawk-claw Jim took all medals. His foremost evil destroyer was hawk claws he had cut off from some hawks that he'd shot. In his pockets were always two or three rabbits' feet. They were invariably left hind feet. He wore a hawk claw on his leather watch chain for a fob. In his old battered sombrero were three hawk feathers—and I've never seen him without this hat even when he went to sleep at night in his blankets.

His greatest achievements was with a rifle. He was what they called in those days a rifleman. Nobody could convince him of the virtues of a Colt or sixgun. He had about the biggest hands I have ever seen on any man before or since. This must have accounted for his prowess with a Winchester because he could do almost anything that you could do with a sixgun. I've seen him walk or ride along with the rifle in his big right paw and snap a shot at a prairie dog or coyote or bird and shoot the eyes out of the varmint without taking aim. A rifle was his whole existence. He believed you could do anything with a rifle and he come the closest of doing it, too. He was never very far from that rifle either, even when eating; and consequently nobody give him much trouble.

He ran into all kinds of trouble when coming to a town. They'd in some places try to bar him from entering the town with his rifle. Other towns wouldn't let him enter a saloon with the rifle. If he'd get mad, almost always he'd shoot up the town and a few people with it. He wasn't much on society and seemed to figure that a man sooner or later would double-cross him. Perhaps this was the reason he took up with birds and animals. This attitude probably accounts for that big knife scar across the side of his neck and collarbone; maybe caused by a Bowie knife.

Anyway somewhere in his travels he picked up with a crow. He must have found it when it was quite young for he sure had it well trained. He had split its tongue and had taught it a number of words to say. That crow would follow that man everywhere he went. I believe it actually worshiped him. It would alight on his shoulder and playfully peck at his ear when in a loving mood.

While old Hawk-claw was ridin' herd, the crow would idle time away by flying from one cow to the other and eating flies from their backs. That was a good thing that it did. One thing it did eat that wasn't so cute to the rest of the boys was rotten meat or maggots. If we'd chance to be near a dead Indian or coyote, the crow would go over and gorge itself on seasoned meat. Then it'd come back and perch on Hawk-claw's shoulder. This stunt didn't set so well when the boys would be eating dinner, but it never seemed to bother Jim. Also, it made a lot of noise and some of the boys were getting damned tired of the crow. They were for shooting "the black Joe," as they called it—"Joe" was the name Jim affectionately called it.

A number of the boys tried to get the boss to fire Jim. The boss wouldn't hear of it and was of the opinion, I think, that the crow did the herd a lot of good. The boys racked their brain for something to make old Jim leave with his dad-ratted crow. Something you understand that wouldn't make him mad and shoot up a few punchers before he left.

They hit upon the idea of getting Joe, the crow, drunk. First they soaked chunks of sourdough in whiskey and tossed them to the bird. He picked one or two hunks up as if to eat them but soon dropped them as though they were hot potatoes. As a last resort the boys captured black Joe and poured about a tin cup full of whiskey down his gullet whether he liked it or not. You see they did this when old Jim was out punching cows and didn't know it was taking place.

As soon as they got black Joe to swallow that tin cup full they let him go. He was screaming, "Jim! Jim!" I'm telling you as long as I live and breathe that was the funniest sight I ever saw. I and one of the other boys managed to ride near where Jim was when the crow got to him.

Joe was beginning to feel the whiskey when he neared Jim's shoulder. He overshot his calculations and he missed the shoulder perch by a good foot, all the time hollering Jim's name. He flew on about twenty-five feet more before he could wheel around and get started back. He fairly beat the air with extra flapping. When he did arrive, he just dropped like a feather duster into Jim's lap.

By this time Jim had realized that something was wrong with Joe. Jim picked the crow up and smoothed out his feathers and talked to him. He noticed that Joe couldn't stand up very well. Jim spurred his horse and with the crow in one hand galloped back to camp with me and the other fellow right behind him to see the fun. Jim thought that the bird had got some poison. One of the boys didn't care much what Jim would do about it and said, "Ah, Joe's all right, Jim. He drank some whiskey there from one of the tin cups by mistake."

You know, old Jim believed that yarn and I think it saved some of us our hides. He sat the black bird on the ground and tried to sober Joe up. Joe, the crow, would stagger around using his wings as supports croaking "Jim" in a pitiful manner. Every now and then he'd hiccough and I think this caused about everybody to roar with laughter. I say everybody except old Hawk-claw Jim. He was stone faced as ever. He was awed and dumbfounded to think the crow would do such a foolish thing. Joe would just about get himself balanced and steadied down when his eyes would start to close because of the sleepiness effect of the alcohol. Then one of those blasting hiccoughs would cut loose and almost blast his head off. He would have to start all over again of spreading out his wings and bracing his feet to get his balance. I'm sayin' it was the funniest sight I ever saw.

Well, we got our wishes fulfilled by causing old Hawk-claw Jim to leave us with Joe, the crow. Jim was peeved—I could see that— but not knowing the actual facts he marked it all up to the treacherous white man. One morning he and the crow rode out of camp and I've never seen them since.

Source: Charles B. "Charlie" Simmons of Billings, Montana. At the time of this interview, Mr. Simmons, an old-time bronc buster, was seventy-four years old. Apparently, he swore "up and down" to his interviewer that the above story was the "bald truth."
Collector: Chet M. Simpson

POKER-PLAYING MAGPIE

I used to get a kick out of a puncher who had a trained magpie around an outfit I worked on once. This puncher was possessed with an idea that he could teach this magpie to play poker. I believe that the bird made some better plays then he did at that for he was generally losing all his money at the game. He'd get that magpie and spread a blanket out and get a deck of cards. He'd shuffle the deck and deal it a hand as well as himself. It'd hold the cards in one foot and look at 'em and look at 'em and then try to peck the spots off the cards. The puncher had split its tongue and he had taught it to say, "Royal Flush, Four Aces," or "Four Kings," etc. That didn't mean it knew how to play poker. He wouldn't give up, though, he kept trying to teach the dumb mag.

Well, it kept making dumb plays and hopping around on one foot and looking at his hand; so one day he gave it up. He then proceeded to teach it rummy, which the magpie got to play pretty good. What dummy couldn't play rummy?

Anyhow what I'm gettin' to is the disaster caused by teaching this dumb magpie how to play poker in the first place. It was his undoing later on.

The puncher would take the magpie with him to town when

he took a notion to have a drink and gamble a little. One day he was packing the mag on his shoulder in a saloon and showing off how smart he was at teaching birds to talk. When he'd entertained the boys as much as he had taught the magpie, somebody wanted him to take a hand at poker. Okay, he would do that little thing. He sat down and played and played. The mag sat on his shoulder and never let a peep out. It'd look everybody over and look at the hands he was drawing and then maybe preen a feather or two to pass away the time. Finally the puncher drew a hand that caught the eye of the magpie. The mag stretched his neck out and looked at the hand again, first with one eye and then with the other. Then he yelled, "Four Kings! Four Kings!" The hell of it was, it was the truth.

The stakes were over two thousand dollars and the puncher couldn't afford to let anybody know what he had in his hand. He tried to pass the magpie's remark off as a joke, but the sharpie who was left playing against the puncher knew better. Anyway the man called him and won the pot.

The puncher was so mad at that magpie that he could kill it. He reached around and grabbed the mag and threw the poor bird clear across the saloon and into a spittoon. The mag crawled out covered from bill to tail with tobacco juice. He was a pitiful sight. He walked sheepishly out the back door and hopped up on a fence post and began cleaning himself up.

The puncher forgot about the magpie and went at the poker game again. I walked out the back way of the saloon and was observing the mag. As I got out there, a sow came grunting along the fence post. She was plastered with mud having recently wallowed in a mud hole.

The magpie stretched his neck and looked and looked the old sow over. Finally he bust out, "Aha! You've been playing poker too."

Source: Charles B. "Charlie" Simmons of Billings, Montana. At the time of this interview, Mr. Simmons, an old-time bronc buster, was seventy-four years old.
Collector: Chet M. Simpson

DUMB HORSE

I had a team of horses around the year '93 and one of 'em was the dumb-est creature that ever lived. He never did anything easy and he had a perfect genius for finding the dumbest way to do it. He was a pretty dappled gray and the first look you took of him you couldn't help but say a good word for him or remark what a wonderful horse he was. His hide was always sleek and he had a way of carrying his head that made him look proud. I don't know what he had to look proud about unless it was some of the dizzy performances he put on.

The prize dumb stunt he put on was one time I decided to go to Billings with the team to get a load of lumber. In those days you had to be ferried across the Yellowstone River near what is now Laurel, Montana. The only way you could get your horses across was to swim them across. I took the other horse and swam him across the river in high style and there wasn't any bother much. The dappled gray, the dummy, was for going across the river in great haste because he could see the other horse on the other side of the river. In fact that was my strategy, to take the smartest one over first and maybe that would induce the other one to get enthused.

Well, it did but that is as far as it went. As soon as the dappled gray got going about twenty feet or more out into the river he got scared. He swam the goofiest of any swimming horse I ever saw. All that stuck out of the water while he swam was his nose, eyes, and ears. I've never seen another horse swim just like that but leave it to the dappled gray to pick that way of doing it. Of course I followed alongside of him on the steamboat. He spied the boat and made right for it. The owner of the ferryboat saw him and tried to get out of his way, but he came up so fast that we couldn't get the boat out of the way in time.

What does the fool do but try to climb into the boat. He gets both front feet over the side and the owner starts hollering to me to keep him out of the boat. I had his bridle and halter in my hands and I proceeded to beat him over the head with them. It did no good for he laid his ears back and squealed pitifully and kept on a-comin'. Before I knew it he was in the boat and had walked over to the cabin and was trying to get inside the cabin through the door. The owner was fit to be tied and was yellin' at me to do something for he was about half-scared of the horse and knew we'd be swamped in a few minutes. Water was comin' over the sides at the least little side sway and my feet were soaked.

I rushed over to whip the dumb critter off of the boat and there he was sitting on his hind haunches in front of the cabin door and leisurely yawning and shaking the water out of his ears. The only thing that saved us from going under was the fact that the owner of the boat had put on tremendous speed and we made the other shoreline in time. The ferryboat captain had to run her aground to save the boat.

The dizzy dappled gray knew I was mad enough at him to kill him and when he saw we were so close to shore, he leaped off the boat deck in a flash and calmly waded to the dry bank in knee deep water. He nickered around the other horse and enjoyed his boat ride, and I guess was telling in horse language how he had pulled the wool over my eyes.

I had to help the ferryboat owner to bail out his boat and offered him, in addition to a good stipend I gave him for all of his trouble, to shoot the dappled gray immediately. He wouldn't listen to it and said to forget it. The horse was later stolen by the Crow Indians, and I never lifted my little finger to get him back.

Source: E. L. *"Dick" Grewell of Billings, Montana. At the time of this interview, Mr. Grewell was seventy-one years old, a retired rancher, and had lived in Montana for fifty-two years.*
Collector: Chet M. Simpson

Good Horse Sense

*T*he writer recalls to mind that, along in the spring of 1916, a man from Minnesota came to Prairie County and started a small ranch. He brought with him seven head of eastern-bred horses, consisting of six mares and one registered Percheron stallion, which were all very fine individuals. He raised quite a number of colts from these mares in the years that followed. As time went on, two of these mares developed extraordinary intelligence—one of them being a Standard Bred Hambiltonian, or hot blood as they are called nowadays, and the other one was a Welsh pony. This pony's first colt happened to be a mare and was about the liveliest thing you ever saw.

This man not knowing much about the Western ways or just how things should be carried on, decided that perhaps he might learn something from someone that had been here for a while. So he hired a young cowboy by the name of Bud Rogers to work for him. Bud was of a slow-go-easy nature, but had had some experience in the Western ways. Bud worked for this man some over twenty years, and is now operating the ranch by himself, after taking unto himself a wife.

After this pony colt grew to be about three years old and it was time to break it to ride, Bud said, "You know boss, we all gonna make the best cow hoss out of that pony that there is in all Prairie

County." The second day at riding this pony (of course she only weighed eight hundred pounds), Bud rode out in the pasture to look after some young hiefers that were having their first calves. He came across one of them that just wouldn't let her calf have anything to eat, so Bud said to his pony, "Well Nellie, looks like here is some new work for you." (The pony had been named Nellie the first day after she was born.) Bud took down his rope and dropped it around the young cow's neck and snubbed her up to the saddle horn. Then he said to his pony, "Now it's up to you to hold this critter while that calf and I do some milking." She sure did her part in the game. When the calf was about through milking, its mother, thinking it about time to go, made a wild lunge to get away, but Nellie just reached over with her teeth and took Mother Cow by the ear, as much as to say, "No, you don't."

One other time about two years later, Nellie displayed her knowledge by using good horse sense. This was one day when the men were all away from the ranch and did not expect to return until late in the evening. As was usually the case when they were to be away, Nellie was left at home as she was trusty for the women folks. Toward evening when it was cow time, Mrs. Minnesota-man's wife went to the corral where Nellie had been taking it easy all day. She opened the gate and said to Nellie, "I'm not feeling good today, so it's up to you to bring the milk cows home by yourself." So Nellie trotted off, seemingly in very good spirits to think she could go by herself. In about an hour she returned with all five milk cows, and also the papa cow. When the Missus closed the gate she wondered, and when she told her husband about it that evening, he only laughed and said, "Well, when Nellie was put in the corral this morning, Bud made the remark that whoever went for the cows that evening should bring the papa cow along for he was to be transferred to another pasture the next day."

Source: Fred Like

Dog Gone Loco!

Wayndle: *Out with it, Tex, I know damned well you've got a tale on your mind, settin' there with a grin on your puss like a cat that's put away both the two goldfish and topped it off with the canary.*

[*Tex Irvine glanced up from where he was setting on a chair out in front of the Belt Shoe Repair Shop, his aged eyes atwinkle at my brusque manner. After a few moments he replied.*]

Tex: I was just laughin' about Buck Rogers. Your wantin' dog stories made me think of Buck Rogers.

Wayndle: Tex, at your age you surely don't read the funny papers. If you're not careful you'll have me believing there is something to this second childhood stuff.

Tex: Funny papers, funny papers: I don't get 'ya, I thought your mind's gone to the dogs.

Wayndle: I see, Tex, you really don't understand. You see there's a character in the funny papers by the name of Buck Rogers—he's a sort of a miracle man who can do things that no one else can do.

Tex: That sounds just about like the Buck Rogers I knew, but I didn't meet him in the funny papers. The first time I saw him it was about five o'clock one morning down at Miles City. It was my first day there; I'd just come from Texas to this country. I was lookin' for a place to get me my breakfast when I run into him. He was walkin' around in his sock-feet, bare-headed, and carryin' one boot in his hand:

"Hey, Jake," he says to me, "where in the god-damned hell is Bessie's place?" "Bessie, Bessie," I says, "I don't know no Bessie.

I'm just a stranger in these parts. What's the matter, yer corns hurt?"

"No, damn it to hell my corns don't hurt!" he snaps back. "I'd look crazy as hell runnin' around here with only one shoe on, wouldn't I?"

I tells him that he don't look like he's over burdened with brains runnin' around at daybreak kickin' over horse walnuts in his bare feet.

"Naw, it's this-a-way, Jake,—"

"My name's not Jake." I said. One of the dirtiest curs I ever knowed was named Jake, and it didn't set any too darned well when anybody called me Jake.

"All right, Sam Houston, all right. I know that name won't tetch ye too much; I know damned well that you're a 'Lone Star' buzzard, although it's gettin' harder and harder to tell you fellers since they started de-hornin' the cattle down there before they bring 'em up here. Come and help me find Bessie's. My dog's there."

I wasn't sure whether I should go with him or not, but I was kinda anxious to start gettin' acquainted up here as I intended to stay in Montana if I could find anything to do. I said, "Dontcha think it'd be better that you find yer other boot before you look for yer dog? If the dog's smart he'll find you before you find him."

"Christ-almighty, Tex, if I can find Bessie's, I'll find my boot. And when I find my boot, I'll find my dog because he's layin' down by it thinkin' I've rolled in with the other one on. He's a smart dog, he knows that the ladies'd think I was a hell of a guy if I crawled in with both boots on."

"How come you leave Bessie's with only one boot?" I asked.

"I go out to take a obscenity and goes to sleep. When my shirt-tail starts flutterin' in a cold breeze I comes to. I forgets that I'm not still in bed, and when I begins to wake-up I don't remember where I was in bed at. I looks around and all I see is a herd of backdoors that all look alike. I sashays down the alley figurin' that I come around to the front and find out where I'm at. When I hits them plank walks my one boot makes me sound like a one-legged man dancin' a hoe-down with a pregnant squaw. I took the damned thing off and was walkin' around lookin' for Bessie's when I runs into you."

Well, Buck (he'd already told me his name and I'd told him mine) goes on ramblin'. I could see that he was feelin' pretty woozy, so I says to him, "Come, let's go and find a saloon that's open and swiggle a few bourbons."

"By golly, you sure think good, Tex. I think you're a right smart feller all-'round. Maybe we'll run into one o' Bessie's pimps—the dirty obscenities—and get him to show us his heifer's range."

We hit out down the street; Buck hoppin' along in his sock-feet, cussin' all pimps, and especially Bessie's pimp. He'd never seen him, he didn't even know for sure that she had one, but when you're locked out of a joint with only one boot you'll give her credit for havin' a dozen of 'em. We come to a saloon that'd been open all night and goes in. There's a poker game goin' on. Buck goes over to where the players was at, a couple of 'em knowed 'im and they busts out laughin' when they sees what a helluva fix he's in. He argues with 'em a little while and finally one of 'em gets up from the game and comes over to the bar. Buck introduces him to me. He's one of the fellers he'd been workin' with before they'd got paid off the day before. I bought a drink. All the time Buck is chatterin' like a magpie about Bessie havin' more doors in her joint than a Chinese hop joint. It only took about three drinks to get Buck started on the road toward a big bender. Now by all rights I would have left them then and there, but I was new in this country and I wanted to get acquainted, that's why I stuck around. His friend manages to get him started on the trail of his boot and dog. Just as we get out the door we run right smack into a big collie carryin' a boot in its mouth. Just as soon as he saw Buck he runs up and drops the boot at his feet and then jumps up with his front feet on Buck's chest and starts lickin' his face. He sure was glad to find Buck. After pettin' 'im for a few seconds, Buck picks up his boot and sets down on the edge of the boardwalk and rams his hoof into it.

"What the god-damned hell's in this boot?" he yells, at the same time shovin' his hand down in it. When he pulls it out he finds that Bessie had put a half-pint o' bourbon in it for 'im. "Now thare's a real gal for you! I'm sure proud o' that woman. My, my, what a swell wife she'd make; I'd marry 'er in a minute if I was worthy of 'er."

"What about her pimp, don'tcha think he'd have something to say about that?" I ask 'im.

"Who in the hell said she had one of them god-damned obscenities? And you listen here, Tex, we don't stand for anybody sayin' insultin' things about decent women up here even if they are in that kinda business."

Well I stayed with Buck and his friends the rest o' that day. He was sure a funny cowboy. He hated sheep like anybody else who worked cows, yet in lots o' ways he was like a sheepherder. He liked his dog better'n he did his horse, and he sure had a dog to be proud of. That dog was almost human. Buck'd put ten or twelve dimes in its mouth, then he'd hold out a piece of rock candy and ask him what he'd pay for it. The dog'd spit out two dimes, and I don't care how many times you offered him rock candy he'd never jar loose with more'n two dimes. Then they'd get a bone and ask 'im what'd he pay for that? He'd sniff at it, turn it over a few times, sizing it up about like a cattle buyer would size up your cows. Finally he'd spit out four dimes. Buck'd say, "No, I gotta have five dimes for that bone." The dog'd drop his dimes to one side and re-examine the bone and decide it wasn't worth more'n four dimes. He'd look at Buck and bark his protest against such robbery. When

Buck wouldn't give in, the dog would gather up his big pile o' dimes and the four that he'd offered for the bone and go over in a corner; all the time eyein' the bone, but never attemptin' to take it. It was quite a sight watchin' him pick his dimes up off the floor. He'd take his foot and spread 'em out so that they'd be about six inches apart. After he'd get 'em that way he'd make a swack at one of 'em with his long tongue. Sometimes he'd do it so fast that the dime would spin in the air, but he'd catch it in his mouth before it'd get to the floor. He'd store each dime away in the side of his jaw like a chipmunk would a hickory nut. Sometimes there'd be a slip and the whole batch of them would fall out on the floor. He'd patiently go to work gatherin' 'em up until he had 'em all stored away in the side of his jaw. I still don't know how he could separate three or four dimes and yet not drop the rest of 'em. They'd get the dog in the crowd and try to fool him by tryin' to peddle him cigars, whiskey or beer, but he'd pay them no attention a-tall. After a while, Buck saw a good lookin' woman go by the front of the saloon, and he yells, "Hey, Bob, what'd y' give for that baby?" The dog'd look at Buck pointin' at the woman then he'd spit out all the dimes, they'd roll all over the floor, he'd start barkin' and jumpin' around like a stallion. Goddamn, but it was funny.

Wayndle: How long, Tex, did you stick along with your friend, Buck Rogers?

Tex: We never worked together at all, but nearly every place I went I would run into him, or someone who knowed him by his dog. About five years after I'd met him, and while I was workin' here in the coal mines in Belt, I dropped into Andy Belevir's saloon and found him in there soundin' off. He was glad to see me if for no other reason than to guy me about givin' up wranglin' for the coal mines. I asked him where Bob his dog was.

"Hell, ain't you heard yet? The son-of-a-bitch went loco on me over at Lewistown last year."

"No, I ain't heard," I told him. "But I ain't surprised a bit, with him havin' to hang around you. How'd it happen?" Then Buck started into a long tale about how Teddy Blue (Abbott) had give him a job for awhile. I think Teddy Blue gave the dog the job and just tolerated Buck. The dog was darned good show for the kids. "What about Bob's goin' crazy?" I asks.

"Why, Teddy Blue," Buck says, "tells me to go out and cull out the best of his three-year-olds as he wants to send 'em into Billings in a couple o' days. Bob and me, and a damned crazy barb pony I had, starts out early figurin' that I could easily do it in a day. Bob was actin' funnier 'en hell. Every time I'd get near him he'd snarl at me and run off to the side. I thought he was sick from something he'd ate as he'd puked his guts up the night before. I didn't have much time to worry about him because I had to do the job all by myself. It'd of been easy if he'd of been actin' all right, but he was doin' more harm than good. About noontime I takes my feed bag from behind the saddle and sets down underneath a cottonwood to eat. All the time Bob's a-millin' around like he's got crabs on his tail. That was kinda funny because he always knowed that when I ate, he ate, yet he don't come over to dinner. All at once, hell pops wide open in that herd. I jumps up to see what the hell it's all about, and there I saw Bob jumpin' from one steer to another, bitin' and snarlin', and the cattle all goin' loony. I hollers my fool head off at him, but he don't pay me no-never-mind. I hops a-straddle my pony and heads toward him. When I get up close he makes a dive at my horse. It was so quick I hardly had time to see it, but the horse did, and in jumpin' out o' the way he damned near set me on the ground. 'I'll rope the bastard,' I says to myself. I said it all right, but that's as close as I ever come to ropin' 'im. Why that son-of-a-gun was harder to rope than tryin' to rope a bumblebee. After runnin' around in circles awhile he just keels over. I goes up to him and his mouth looks like it was the foam on the top of a pail of warm fresh milk. I knows then that the bastard's balmy, so I plugs 'im. I lets the cows go to hell and heads back to tell old Abbott what's happened. Before I was halfway through tellin' 'im I begins to think that I was goin' to have to plug him too; he was foamin' and frothin' damned near as bad as Bob did. 'Get to hell back out there and head every cow toward the house. I'm going into Lewistown and get the vet.' I had 'em pretty close to the pens when he and the doc get there. The doc says we got to examine every damned one of 'em and put the bitten ones off all by theirselves. It was a hell of a job. Them damned critters acted like they was virgins and they thought I was no gentlemen. By eight o'clock we'd gone over 'em all and we found there was four that'd been bit. The Doc had us pen each one of 'em in a pen by hisself and wait and see what happens. By golly, they wait for about three weeks and was just about ready to turn 'em out with the herd when, bang! one young heifer starts hoppin' around like she's got cockroaches in her udder. She's bellowin' and jumpin' up, and settin' down and jumpin' up and settin' down; her mouth looking like she'd drunk a can o' beer and all the foam was caught on her mustache. Old Abbott goes and gets his buffalo gun and hands it to me and yells at me like the heifer, 'You kill'er, you made 'er that way!' 'Sure, you betcha,' I says, and I sends her on her merry way to join Bob. After that Teddy Blue sends me into Lewistown for the Doc to come out. When we get back he looks over the mess and says that we got to kill the other three as they might go looney durin' the night and break out. Again I'm handed the buffalo gun and evertime I shoot it it damn near knocks my shoulder three feet back of my hind end. The next day Teddy Blue tells me that he knows where there's a damned good range for me to work, it's a place just suited for me so he's gonna gimme my pay right now so's I can get an early start.

I takes the cart-wheels and asks where this good range is to be found. 'It's over in Hades, Buck,' he says. 'How d'ya get there?' I asks 'im. 'Goddamnit, Buck, you've been on your way over there since the day you was born. Just ask anybody in Lewistown and they'll show you the way.'"

"When I gets to Lewistown I asks around where Hades is. Finally George Ayers tells me. That god-damned old bastard of a Teddy Blue Abbott knew all the time that Hades was in Hell."

Source: Nathan S. "Tex" Irvine of Belt, Montana. Mr. Irvine came to Montana from Texas in 1891.
Collector: Wayndle R. Johnson

THE NEWFOUNDLAND AND THE TERRIER

William Berkin and family were living at the Gaffney stage station between Whitehall and Alder in 1877. Tom Berkin's brother-in-law, George LaPoint, who was an expert horseshoer, was away at the time. Tom Berkin was about eight years old. Early one morning he went out horseback to get a saddle mare. He had a big Newfoundland dog and a small terrier dog with him. He hadn't been out long when a blizzard struck. Tom's hat blew off and he got off his horse, threw the bridle reins over a fence post and went after his hat. In a short time Tom lost his way in the fierce blizzard and he fell into a spring. His clothes were soon frozen and he kept going until he was exhausted. The horse got loose and went home. Thirteen men went out hunting for Tom. It was through the aid of the big Newfoundland dog that Tom was found. The dog led one of the stage drivers to where Tom was. The big dog had carried rye grass and had Tom almost covered and the little dog was lying on his chest when the men picked him up. Tom recalls that the men hollered to the others when they found him.

They drew whiskey out of a barrel and saturated the snow in a wash tub with whiskey to thaw out Tom's arms, legs and hands. It was the little dog's warmth and the help of the big dog that saved Tom's life.

Source: *Tom Berkin of Roundup, Montana*
Collector: *Evelyn M. Rhoden*

SPORT

Well, to begin my story, I come west to Montana from Pennsylvania in 1882, and got me a job herding sheep for Thomas Cruse who owned a big ranch near the town of Grass Range. This place was called the N-Bar Ranch, and let me tell you it sure was a big outfit. When I signed up on the payroll there was about one hundred other men—cowboys, sheepherders and cooks. Well, herding sheep was my profession and I was a good herder too. My father who was born in the old country had been a sheepman and had learned me all there was to know about sheep and their care. He told me that the best friend a man could ever have was a good dog and that a good sheep dog depended on the way you trained it. He told me how to teach a dog to fetch certain sheep out of a flock and how to put the sheep in a pen. Well, I learned all about the training of dogs and I trained many a sheep dog in my day. The best dogs for sheep dogs are Shepard and Collie. They seem more smarter than other dogs for this business and learn the tricks faster.

Mr. Cruse was a fine man and although he had a full crew of men when I came along, he gave me a job herding sheep and paid me sixty dollars a month and board. I guess I worked for Mr. Cruse about ten years and in all that time we never had an argument. He liked me very much and raised my pay after he saw that I knew how to herd sheep with the best of them. What he liked most though, was my sheep dog, Sport. Sport was as smart as a whip and didn't have to be told what to do at any time, unless it was to bring in a certain sheep or something like that.

When I got Sport, he was just a pup about two weeks old. I got him from a man in Benton for nothing. Well, I brought Sport up on a bottle and he growed to be a big dog. I never once whipped or scolded him and I would have beat hell out of anyone who ever tried to abuse him or make him afraid. No one ever did. Everyone liked the dog and treated him with kind words and pets. He loved kids and never bit anyone in his life.

Sport died a hero's death at the age of five and half years and was given a swell burial by Mr. Cruse and even had a tombstone with the words, "Here lies the greatest sheep dog that ever lived. Born in 1882, Died in 1887 from wounds received from a pack of hungry coyotes while trying to save the lives of six baby lambs." I never missed anything so much in my life as I missed that dog after he died. He was like a son to me. He followed me wherever I went unless he was told to tend the sheep and he would take as good a care of the sheep as any man could.

Well, when Sport was three months old, I started in training him to be a sheep dog. I took him out to the sheep pasture every morning and started him in with a small band of six sheep. I pointed out each of the six sheep and gave each a name. The dog soon learned to know each of the six sheep and would bring any one of them at my order or all of them, whatever I asked him to do. After awhile, he got so I didn't have to name the ones I wanted. I just pointed to the one I wanted and he would get that one. I taught him not to scare a sheep by barking at it and also not to rush the sheep, but to take it easy and let the sheep have its own way unless the sheep tried to make a break for freedom. In that case, I taught Sport to be quick and bring the sheep back. After he learned to do this, I kept adding more sheep to the flock and before long, Sport was as good with a large flock as he was with just a few sheep. I had a lot of chances to sell the dog but to part with Sport was like cutting off my arm and giving it away. I always refused the offers but I did train dogs for other sheepmen and herders and never charged them nothing for it—because I loved dogs and they loved me I guess, because I never had no trouble in training them.

Well, to get back to the story of why Sport was such a good and faithful dog. It was during the winter of 1886–1887 that he earned the reputation he had. We was out about fifteen miles from the main ranch and only had a camp wagon. All was fine until about November. Then hell busted loose and it got colder than the hinges of hell. The mercury went to about fifty below zero and the sheep, all bunched together, had a hard time of it keeping warm. Bunched together like that, they couldn't move and many of them froze to death on their feet. My hands and feet were frozen and there was icicles hanging from Sport's fangs, but regardless of the cold weather, our job was to keep the sheep moving and to try and save as many as possible. The spring of 1886 had been nice but the hay crops were not sufficient to take care of all the stock and there had been a large number of lambs that spring. Well, not having enough hay to eat, the sheep and lambs did not have enough strength to pull through that winter. Sport and me finally got the sheep to moving and we moved them to the foothills of the Judith

Mountains where more shelter from the winds could be had. Even at that, there were very few sheep left in 1887 and no lambs at all. It was just turning spring of 1887 and the snows were melting fast, causing little rivulets to join together and make swollen streams. Many of the sheep that had pulled through the winter were drowned in the streams because they didn't have the strength to swim out. Sport saved several of the smaller lambs from drowning by swimming out and pulling them to shore.

But that isn't the way Sport got his reputation as being faithful. No, he got his reputation by trying to save some lambs from a coyote pack and I think he would have done it too, if he hadn't been so weak and gaunt from the past winter. It happened that I had run out of grub and had to go to the N-Bar to get some supplies. I told Sport to stay with what sheep were left and watch them until I got back. I knew that they were starved and weak and that the coyotes were fat from eating frozen sheep and cattle and that they would not hesitate to attack a lone dog when there was fresh meat to be had. But I figured on being back before the night set in and I knew that coyotes would be most liable to attack at night. Well, it happened that I did not get back that night. It was in the afternoon of the next day before I got back. I did not see the sheep or dog anywhere. I saw the camp wagon so I figured that the dog had taken the sheep down into a valley where they could get better grass to eat. After I had stored my supplies in the camp wagon and kindled a fire, I started off in the direction of where I thought Sport had taken the sheep. I kept calling and thought it funny that Sport did not come running or at least answer my call.

Then I saw something that almost turned my stomach. I had just went over a hogback when I noticed some of the sheep, banded together and afraid to move in one direction or the other. A little ways off, I saw the remains of six baby lambs, which had been slaughtered by coyotes. I walked down to where they were laying but did not see anything of my dog and I got sick down in my stomach when I thought of what might have happened. I kept calling to him but he did not come or bark and then I knew to be true what my instinct told me. My dog was dead. I walked a little further and entered a small clump of brush and suddenly I came upon what was left of Sport. Well, I just sat down and cried like a baby. Sport was to me like a son to a father. I had raised him from a tiny pup and he knew all of my moods and I knew his. We got along just like a couple of people and never once did he ever let me down.

But Sport had not died alone. No sir, there all around him were dead coyotes, their throats ripped to shreds. Sport had killed four of the animals before being killed himself, and all in his line of duty. I had taught him to protect his sheep with his life and he had not failed me.

Now, every time I think of Sport, I can't help getting tears in my eyes, as you can probably see, but I'll bet you would do the same thing.

Source: William Buchanan, Jr.

A RODENT SPARTACUS

A cat may look at a king, but a rat can shoot up his castle.
The feline right, which has been proudly handed down from generation to generation, first gained recognition centuries ago by the exploit of the immortal "Puss-In-Boots." But it remained for an ordinary Montana mountain rat to demonstrate an even greater possibility.

The "king" was William Hackney, Montana pioneer stockman and miner and for years the monarch of all he surveyed in the Huckleberry and Gleason Gulch district of the upper Nevada

Creek Valley. It was in his cabin where the event occurred that will reverberate down the halls of time until the last rat trap is sprung and the last bit of bait molded away.

Long before the first white man made his appearance in this part of the world, the mountain pack rats had borne with proverbial patience the yoke of oppression. Although they made nocturnal forays on the caches and food supplies of other denizens of the silent places, they never rioted or attempted open warfare. Diligent search of the most ancient archives fails to reveal any occasion when they even went so far as to petition a legislative body for redress of grievances.

It is true they squealed with indignation and tail-pounded the floors and rafters when their troubles became almost too great to bear, but it came to naught until a leader was born in Bill Hackney's domain.

This rat in question had been bothering "King Bill" until he finally lost patience, and loaded an old Zulu model shot gun, which he kept in his cabin as protection against Indians and whites possessed of an insatiable appetite for bug juice. Bill hung the weapon within reach of his bunk, which was constructed in one corner of the cabin. Diagonally across the shanty in the opposite corner was Bill's china closet, of which he was mighty proud. This was constructed of three cracker boxes, one above the other. His cook stove, of the old-style, two-door oven, was directly in the center of the room, midway between the closet and bunk.

Bill was suddenly awakened from his sleep one night by the antics of the rats, which had burrowed their way into the place. Drawing himself out of the blankets to a sitting posture, he spotted the eyes of the critter on the opposite side of the room. Grasping his shotgun, he took aim. The rat was only twelve feet distance. There was no chance of missing and the rat knew it. He closed his eyes and waited. His heart choked his throat and the blood throbbed in his brain.

It was a tense moment—one of those the fiction writers refer to as psychological. As Bill squinted along the barrel, he suddenly became aware that the gleam of the rat's eyes had vanished. The wise old rat had simply closed his eyes, but Bill didn't know. It was one of those threads upon which the destiny of whole races are suspended, and it was snapped by the scissors of capricious destiny. Bill put down the shotgun and got out of bed to light a candle. He wanted to make sure of locating the object of his previous aim.

As he scratched a match on the side of his bunk, the rat opened his eyelids and the strength that terror had drained from his body increased ten-fold by the stimulus of relief. An ordinary rat would have availed himself of the opportunity offered and go his way rejoicing, in the chance that had snatched him from the closing jaws of death.

But this was no ordinary rat. In him metempsychosis had played a strange trick. Instead of the soul of one of the drab, timid humans, who according to old Indian legends became coyotes and mountain rats when they die, the spirit of a liberator and leader had passed into this particular rat. A Spartucus, a Bolivar, a General Houston was imprisoned in that little body.

He raised his head and dedicated his life to liberty. Then he jumped directly at the trigger of Hackney's cocked shotgun, lying on the bunk. There was a roar that caused the cabin to rock on its foundation logs, and a charge of double-B8s whistled through the folds of Bill's *robe de nuit*, lifted the open oven door off the cook stove and hurled it kersmash against the china closet. There was a crash of dishes and the interior of the cabin took on the semblance of an inferno from the smell of burning black powder.

For a moment Bill was unable to determine if he was shot, wounded or had exploded, but it was soon apparent he was in the same position as the doughboy who wandered into a cloud of mustard gas in the front line trenches. Drunkenly he made his way in the general direction of the door coughing and spitting. Once he was outside and in the open, his mind began to function normally. While still at a loss to understand the situation, Bill recalled it was a single shot, fired by a fanatic at Sarejevo, that brought on World War No. I, and for all he knew it might have only been a lifted eyebrow, a hand touched in passing, or a playful kiss in Menelaus' garden that was responsible for the strife between the Greeks and Trojans.

It was not until daylight arrived that Bill surveyed the interior of his wrecked castle. Then he was able to comprehend that the shot fired by the rat had sounded through ratland. The hour had struck and the rats were on the scamper. There was revolt in the vicinity of Bill Hackney's cabin. A Moses had been found to lead the packrats to the land where leather goods and such delicacies as stockmen's boots grew, and where cowmen and prospectors who pulled shotguns on poor defenseless rats were turned into pillars of bacon for even looking at rodents or saying things about them.

One of the things that stirred the patriotic propensities of the pack rats, that mobilized with triumphant squeaks about Bill's cabin the next night, was that the shot fired in defense of their rights had come from the enemy's gun.

Source: Si Stoddard of Anaconda, Montana, claimed to have learned the story above from a stockman named Kersinger in 1910.

FEATHERED RETRIEVER

*D*on't tell me the hawk is a predatory bird," *exclaimed old Elgee Smith, as he tossed the morning paper to one side, and pumped a mouthful of tobacco juice at a blue-bottle fly that was inspecting the moist spot where the previous discharge of saliva had landed.* "These so-called experts of natural history may think they are fooling folks, but old Elgee isn't one of them. I know what I'm talking about, because I saw it with my own eyes."

Elgee's reputation for veracity has never been questioned. This may be attributed to the fact that the old fellow stands well over the six-foot mark, and is rather handy in knowing how to make his fist do considerable damage. Perhaps there are folks who might regard him in the same manner Teddy Roosevelt did the nature fakers, but regardless, he is entitled to a full set of Dresden china decoys for his latest. Elgee backed up his claim with the following story:

It happened last fall during the duck hunt I made down at Red Rock. I was standing on a reed-covered point, flanked on both sides by open water. It was an ideal blind, except for the fact the dead ducks flopped into the open water, which was too deep for wading. To retrieve the ducks a boat was necessary, and I had no boat. I decided to shoot, however, until I neared the limit, then wait for the wind to shift and blow my ducks in shore.

The first bird to come along was a greenhead, and I let him have it. As he landed ker-plunk in the open water, I broke my gun to extract the empty shell. While so engaged I chanced to glance toward the dead duck, and was stupefied to see a gigantic hawk swoop down, seize it in his claws and fly off. I followed its line of flight, and saw it alight on a bluff about a quarter-mile away. Just about this time a second duck came sailing in so I let him have it.

It was while I was reloading that I again heard the swish of wings. There was that darned hawk again, ready to lift the dead duck out of the water. I raised my gun to shoot, but a happy thought caused me to change my mind.

"Why should I kill that hawk?" I considered. I'll let him retrieve my ducks, then climb up to the nest and take them.

Then the ducks began to come in. The shooting was splendid and the old hawk stayed on the job. As soon as I downed one, the hawk would swoop over it, pick it up and head for his nest. As I picked my tenth webfoot out of the air, I shouldered my gun and started for the hawk's nest. There they lay, every one of them. But that's not all.

While that old hawk was busy carrying the dead birds to her nest, her trio of fledglings had pulled off every feather of the birds that comprised the bag. With the exception of being drawn, those birds were ready for the oven.

Source: Si Stoddard of Anaconda, Montana

BULL TAKES POSSESSION OF A CABIN

*V*irtue had employed some men to burn brick near his ranch. He built a cabin for the men to batch in and had it well stocked with provisions for the men.

A severe storm came, and the men all went to town, imbibed quite freely with liquid refreshments and did not return to the cabin for two or three days.

The wind evidently blew the door open, and a large bull had taken refuge from the storm in the cabin, and the door had become closed in some manner, and the "old bull" had full possession.

Smithy went to the cabin to see how the men were faring, and on approaching the cabin, heard quite a commotion. On opening the door, there were no men, but a big old bull, instead, who had literally wrecked the provisions and furnishings. He had evidently tackled a fifty-pound sack of flour. His horns had penetrated the sack; the bull was unable to extricate the sack from his horns and it covered his entire head.

Smithy gave a war hoop on seeing the animal, and it lunged through the only window in the cabin.

The old man, Tom Mason, who had charge of the cabin and crew, was an old scotch sailor who had rounded Cape Horn on an old sailing vessel, sailed up the coast to California, and had experienced many severe storms on salt water. He remarked that he never saw such a damned wreck, as that bull had made of his cabin.

Source: Harry Smith related this story of an incident that took place on the Virtue Ranch.
Collector: C. E. Thompson

THE SELF-RELIANT MARE

A horse belonging to one gentleman learned to be very self-reliant. Here's the story, and though it does seem odd, there are many ready to prove it. As tractors were not very common at this time and the man in question did a great deal of farming, he naturally owned quite a few horses.

The custom was, when returning from the fields at noon, to unhitch the horses at the barn. Then, with their harnesses jingling, they would follow the driver down to the pump, where water was pumped for the thirsty bunch. As the water pumped very easily no windmill was necessary, he thought.

One very hot summer day the horses were unhitched and trooped off to the pump. Now, the farmer was detained with something at the barn, and when the horses reached the trough there was no water. So one old mare, that had watched the water pumping for years, strolled up to the pump, grabbed the handle with her mouth and pumped water for herself and the rest of the horses. She didn't stop with that either, but thereafter she never bothered anyone when she wanted a drink, but always pumped her own water. I believe this is the only case ever heard of where a horse pumped water for itself.

Source: Ruth Lewis

JERRY, A MULE WITH INTELLIGENCE

*J*erry was a mule with intelligence which he used to his own advantage. He had a technique for opening gates, which no one seemed to be able to break. He started in with the garden gate, which had a common lift latch. Then after he once knew how good the corn and cabbage were, all kinds of fasteners were tried on the gate, but it took Jerry only a few minutes work to learn the combination. And from bad he went to worse. Next he turned to the vice of opening the pasture gate, letting the horses out of the pasture. He then took to opening the gates into the field and treating his friends to wheat, oats or whatever they wished. Life was never very quiet while Jerry lived, and then, when he finally took sick and died, we paid our due respects to him, but at the same time a sigh was heard, which sounded more like a sigh of relief than sorrow.

Source: Ruth Lewis

THE WISE OLD TABBY

*W*e knew of a cat that raised at least one family of kittens a year. The two children always divided them up and claimed the chosen ones until they were given away or any other fate that befalls cats.

Once the newborn kittens were brought into the house as it was very cold outside, and an old Montana blizzard was raging. The kittens were put in behind the stove and Tabby had a sudden inspiration to divide them up herself. I imagine she thought something like, "Oh, they'll take them anyway, I might as well distribute them myself."

So, she took her four kittens one at a time and gave them out to the two children. But instead of dividing them evenly she made the mistake of giving two to one of the children, one to the other and the fourth one to the mother of the children. The child who felt slighted took the kitten from his mother, but Tabby wouldn't think of such a situation and immediately picked the kitten up and gave it back to the mother.

She was a very wise old cat and this is only one of the intelligent things she did. Maybe she was so thankful to be brought into a nice warm place from the cold that her feline heart just filled with gratitude to such an extent that she was moved to give her little family away.

Source: Ruth Lewis

TONY: AN OLD COW PONY

*S*o *you want a story of an old cow pony.* Gosh, that's a hard one as there were lots of good horses and every fellow thought his own was the best. But I'll tell you about the best one I ever forked. He wasn't long on looks and he wasn't the fastest horse I ever rode, but he was by far the best little fellow who ever trotted the north country range. He was dependable, was old Tony. A little chunky gray fellow, big head, and wise looking, seemed almost like he was clumsy on his feet but he could turn on a dime and was the best rope and cutting horse I ever had. Money couldn't-a bought that horse from me for he saved my life more than once, just by being coolheaded and sure footed. I thought the world of Tony.

I got him from a fellow up north. I was breaking out a bunch of horses for him and he gave me the pick of the lot. I liked his looks so I chose him. They laughed at me as there were many handsomer and faster horses in the bunch, but I figured he was the most intelligent and that's what you want in a cow pony. He was a three-year-old then and had such a funny, wise look, just like a little old man. Soon as he found out what I wanted, he'd follow me anywhere, but he'd also kick up his heels and jump over the yard fence and away when he felt like it.

When he was about four years old I was up near the Canadian line after some horses. It was early in the winter and late in the afternoon when a blizzard struck. My mother was alone on our homestead and we had quite a little bunch of cattle. I figured I'd better hightail it for home. The blizzard with its wind and icy sleet was roaring down upon Tony and me. It came from the southeast so we had to face it all the way. We were almost thirty miles from home. But we started. It kept getting colder and colder and the trail was almost invisible because of the snow and wind. That darned little pony had never been over the road before but he jog-trot-jog-trotted along never missing a gap, steady and sure-footed over steep hills and along cut banks, where if he had slipped we would have fallen to the ice far below. I thought I'd freeze for the ice and sleet stung like needles and I could not see. My face, where it was exposed, felt like it was freezing; my hands and feet were numb. Several times I got off, and clinging to Tony's mane and clutching his bridle, followed on foot where he led, in order to warm up a little. I thought I must be getting close to home, but my eyeballs were frozen and I couldn't see when we brought up smack against a shed door. I heard a door open and Ma's voice said, "Is that you, George?" I was right up against our kitchen door. Ma helped me in, as I couldn't see, and took Tony to the barn, which luckily wasn't far and which was sheltered from the storm by the house. She bedded him and fed him as I couldn't see for three days. After that he was Ma's pet. He had never been handled by a woman before, but after that he'd follow her like a dog.

Tony was the best rope and cutting horse you ever saw. He'd just go right after a critter and nothing could make him quit till he'd get her. And then he'd give a foolish cow a good nip on the hip just to let her know she had better move where he wanted her. Always used his head and nothing rattled him.

"Why, Uncle George," said my little nephew from the city. "You don't have to steer Tony, he just steers himself. I tell him to get the white cow or old Krop ear, and he just does it all himself. Tony's fun."

One time we fellows sort of thought we'd have a polo team just as the play boys did, and we challenged the Missouri River boys to play us a game at the fair. We started practicing with croquet mallets and a croquet ball, but the team sort of broke up after one or two got a crack with a mallet or got bucked off. The worst of it was that the cowboy who rode Tony complained that he went after the ball and picked it up in his mouth. I ain't saying that's so. So the game was indefinitely postponed but I rather think the south fellows didn't accept our challenge.

I did run down a coyote and rope it from Tony's back, but he objected rather strenuously when I tried to bring it home on his back. I could carry a little calf in, but no coyotes for him.

As he grew older, he grew wise to the fact that I rode him too far for his own comfort. So if he could he'd run away, and frolic around just far enough so I couldn't catch him. Finally when I'd begin to use a little mite of bad language he'd let me catch him. When I put my foot in the stirrup, he'd be off like a shot. But when my little daughter was old enough for school, Tony would turn his head, watch until she was firmly seated in the saddle with her school bag and lunch basket, then he'd sigh mournfully and away they'd go, trot, trot, trot. Guess he didn't like to go to school very well. We used to watch for her at night and I liked to hear her come singing, "Hurry up old fellow, or we'll never get home tonight." That song, "Old Faithful," certainly described Old Tony.

As the years passed, old Tony's hair turned white, and his working days were over too. We just used him for a child's saddle pony. Tony died years ago, but we all feel that if there's a heaven where good horses go, Tony is there where there are sweeter springs and greener pastures, such as his faithful heart deserves.

There were lots better and finer horses owned by the other fellows around for he was only a little old cow pony who did his work well and faithfully.

Source: George P. Miller of Malta, Montana
Collector: Gladys W. Miller

TO GIVE A COW A LESSON

A man named Harris lived near Fairfield with his brother, both bachelors. Harris had been bothered by his neighbor's cattle coming and eating around his haystacks and had warned the neighbor that dire misfortunes would overtake the next bovine critter trespassing on the aforesaid stacks. The neighbor sympathetically agreed that it was too bad, and invited Harris to do his worst—the critters needed a working over anyhow!

Some time later, Harris and a cowboy friend happened to ride up to the haystacks to find the intruder, a decrepit gangling old cow of uncertain age and ancestry, contentedly munching at the nearest stack.

Harris shouted and spurred his horse after the cow while he flourished his rope. The cow waggled her starboard ear and looked around in surprise. Somewhat astonished at Harris's display of energy, she shifted suddenly into high and dashed for the door of a nearby shed. Harris rode up to the door, dismounted, and handed his reins to the cowboy who he directed to hold the door shut while he should go inside and give the old cow a lesson in the form of a beating with the end of his lariat rope. The cowboy did as he was told and propped himself against the door while he listened to the uproar that proceeded from the inside where Harris was giving the old cow a "working over." There was much shouting and bellowing for the first minute or so and then comparative quiet with only an occasional bellow followed by a few indistinct words from Harris. Afraid at last that Harris must have killed the cow, the cowboy opened the door and went inside to view the remains. What was his astonishment to see Harris crowded down into a far corner calling in a voice that had dwindled to little more than a whisper, "Open the door! Open the door!" while the old cow industriously prodded him with her blunted horns. The cow dashed out through the door and Harris was left to examine his bruises while the cowboy doubled up against the wall in unsympathetic mirth.

Source: Elmer Baird of Roundup, Montana

UNNATURAL TALES

Walter Latta with saddled

horse in Bozeman, Montana,

July 1939.

Farm Security Administration,

photo by Arthur Rothstein (#110)

Unnatural Tales

The Devil's Slide

In the Cinnabar Mountains, south of Livingston and not far from Gardiner, is an exposed dike of iron-bearing rock. The dike is visible from US 89 and is on the west side of the Yellowstone River. This exposed rock was called the "Devil's Slide" by early-day settlers. They thought that the red ore exposed was cinnabar and thus named the mountains the Cinnabar Mountains, although there is said to be no cinnabar in the region. The legend has it that the imps of the Devil, and occasionally the Devil himself, used to slide down the "Devil's Slide" and the red coloring to the rocks is caused by the smears of blood left by them. A little ditty, recording the activities of the Devil on this slide, was written by some wag of the early days and runs thus:

Ages ago, one can readily see,
Yellowstone Valley went on a spree;

The mountain had risen and the canyon sunk
And Old Mother Nature got terribly drunk;
The Devil, as drunk as a devil could be,
Slid to the bottom of Cinnabaree.

Source and collector: unknown

SKYSCRAPER BARN

*T*om Halbert built a structure several years ago; he was short of money and timber was scarce. He used willow posts for corner posts and sides, setting them in the ground in a vertical position. The following season he found that the posts had roots and were growing rapidly. That fall, the floor of the barn, which had before been on the ground, was three feet above the ground level. A year ago the barn was on stilts nine feet high and the owner placed another story underneath to conserve space and make entrance easier, making the original one-story barn a two-story structure. Another story has been added this season and the owner had to put in an elevator to take the stock up to the hay. It is only a question of time until the cupola will be looking down over the Snowies into Lewistown. The proprietor contemplates turning the growing structure into a sanitarium. It is certainly one of the strangest freaks that ever developed on Montana soil.

Collector: Evelyn M. Rhoden rewrote this tale from a piece originally printed in the Hedgeville Herald.

THE NAMING OF WHITE BEAVER CREEK

This instance occurred sometime after the establishment of the stage line from Billings to Bozeman. The road then followed the north side of the Yellowstone the full distance, there being no bridges at that time. Naturally taking the route of least resistance the road followed as much as possible the valleys and snuck through the gaps in the hill wherever practicable. The stage stations, while placed as conveniently as possible, were long distances apart, about as far as a stage could go in a day. The stations, while comfortable, were not what the auto tourist would call modern.

The drivers of these stages were all old hands and being lecturers of no mean repute many a long hour was spent wising the pilgrims, dudes, and schoolteachers up to the ways of the country and explaining the various sights seen along the way, some of which required lengthy explanations.

It was on one of these trips that one cowboy, Jack, had a passenger of an eastern girl coming west for the first time to teach in a country school in western Montana. Being an up-and-coming girl, she was riding up front and taking in the country as they went, Jack explaining the various sights as they went.

For several miles they had been following a pretty little stream of no great size but with several interesting sights which Jack explained in great detail. The afternoon waned as they were drawing close to the station known as the Stonehouse. The schoolteacher, much to Jack's embarassment, noticed a white object some distance from the station, as luck would have it, and called for an explanation.

Jack was stumped, but only for a minute. His great experience stood him in good stead. "Ma'am," he said, "That is something that you probably will never have a chance to see again even though you traveled for years in the great outdoors. You are now looking at a white beaver—very rare and practically extinct. It is very easily frightened and we had better not get close."

On arriving at the station and after the girl had gone inside, the driver cornered the caretaker and suggested that he air the chamber pot someplace else besides along the creek in sight of the main stage road. The story got around and that creek and its branches has always been called the White Beaver. The schoolteacher, stage driver and cowboy Jack are gone and almost forgotten, but the Stonehouse is still there and the little creek that flows by it in wet years is still known as the White Beaver.

Source: John Hiner
Collector: Walter L. Roberts

TENT-FLAPPING WINDS

*M*r. A. S. Shannon together with a man by the name of Mr. Hall ran the first drugstore at Coulson, at that time all the stores being located in tents. Whenever a storm came up he had to take all of his goods off of the shelves and put them on the floor so the flapping of the tent would not mix them. One day a big dust storm came up. Mr. Shannon took everything off of the shelves, and when the storm was over he put them all back. He had no sooner gotten them put back when another dust storm came up, and before he could get them off the shelves, a lot of them had gotten mixed. Shortly afterward a customer came into the store and asked for some flaxseed meal to make a poultice for his eyes. An hour later the customer came howling and lamenting into the store, saying that the flaxseed was hot and had burned his eyes out. This was not entirely true, although the flaxseed was indeed hot as it had been mixed with the Cayenne pepper during the dust storm, as investigation proved.

Collector: Edna Felthousen of Billings, Montana

Outrunning a Storm

*T**his rancher had a team of unusually fast horses and one summer afternoon drove this team to town hitched to a wagon.* The wagon had a spring seat up in front and so, of course, the man rode sitting on the spring seat while his dog rode in the wagon box behind. Well anyhow, that afternoon while the man was on his way home from town there came up a big black storm cloud and it began to rain off in the distance behind him a mile or so. He looked back and seeing that it was going to be a regular downpour and having no raincoat with him and having an unusually fast team, he whipped up his horses and gave them their heads to see if he could outrun the storm. But the storm gained quite a bit on him before the horses got into their stride. He could hear the raindrops pattering into the wagon box behind him. He had to give all his attention to guiding the horses down the right trail and could not look back. The horses ran their best and he pulled up at his ranch house congratulating himself that he had escaped the storm, when, looking around, to his amazement he found that the storm had followed him so close that the wagon box was half full of water and his poor dog had had to swim all the way home!

Collector: Elmer Baird of Roundup, Montana

A Windy Day

*S**ure it's windy today.* Not too bad at that. Say, back in twenty-four there really was wind. Not a breeze just like now. I remember, spring of twenty-four, it blowed so hard it started to lift rocks up off the ground. I was breakin' a forty of prairie that was rocky, and I had a tough time. Had to keep my arm in front of my face. At that, I had black eyes from them danged rocks all spring.

Source: John Melrude of Alma, Montana, relayed this anecdote while standing in a wheat field.
Collector: Ralph C. Henry

WILDCAT SPRINGS

*T*hem springs are called Wildcat Springs—an' not because there was a sign of a wildcat there. Away back a couple of cow waddies was down in Shelby celebratin' high an' wide and not repressin' themselves a-tall. One of 'em met a girl an' in record time got engaged to her to the extent of givin' him a picture. Well, towards mornin', she got to figurin' she didn't think so much of this cow waddie, an' takin' stock of the situation as it was, she figured she'd better get rid of him. Which she did, with her fingernails, after which she drawed a gun. This cow waddie I mentioned went hightailin' outa town at high speed, with his partners. Bein' due for work anyway they rid the balance of the night, the which of there wasn't much, an' finally hauled up at Wildcat Springs fer a rest.

The disappointed suitor, after guzzlin' water which was distasteful but necess'ry, no tarantual juice bein' around, felt his head, which was some spinnin'. He felt of his face, which was scratched plum raw. Then he felt of the picture in his pocket, which was addin' insult to injury.

So this aforementioned waddie pulls that picture out, looks at it long an' lamentin'ly, and says, tearin' it to pieces, "You wildcat!" An' since then, them springs have been called Wildcat Springs.

Source: Jack Ryan of Cutbank, Montana
Collector: Ralph C. Henry

UNDER THE INFLUENCE

Cowboys in town for a drinking party after a roundup, April 29, 1942.
Loaned to the WPA by Mrs. Rae Berg of Superior, Montana (#85)

UNDER THE INFLUENCE

NO NOSE

I seed 'bout the horriblest fight in my life right here in Billings in the old days. There was two jaspers thet were partners in a saloon. One was Tim 'n other was Tom. Tim was the business man and Tom was the easy-going cuss. While he's tendin' bar he's giving away more'n he's a-sellin'. Tim would cuss him out plenty and Tom would reform fer a day er two. Then he'd be right back at it again. Finally Tim bought Tom out and told him he was through as a partner. Tom fer spite opened up a saloon across the street from Tim and sed he'd allow he could get all the business. It didn't never work out thet away, fer Tom kept going in the hole every day. The worse Tom's finances got the madder he got at Tim fer his rotten luck and blamed it all on Tim.

It got so bad thet the old pals had swore to kill the other on sight. The sheriff heard about it and went and seed the boys. The sheriff sez, "You boys is brothers under the skin. Jist got some meanness in your hides ye wanta get shed of. Whyn't ye fight it out with fists." Well, the old partners couldn't very well back out.

Everybody gathered to seed the fun. They formed a circle around Tim and Tom right on main street. Son, those jaspers fought fer three hours or more and were pretty well matched. They slugged and smashed each other. The blood flew 'n the teeth flew. I never knew two human beings had so many teeth. Tim would slug 'em in the mush and Tom would step back and spit out blood and teeth, or it was vicy-versy. Both their faces were like raw beef-steaks. When they hit each other in the face it made a swish. They had managed to close each other's eyes pretty even and neither could see very good. A number of the boys wanted them to stop. Nuthin' doin'. They wuzn't so yaller ers thet.

It got so bad thet they could hardly see each other, their eyes were so swollen, and towards the last were wraslin' each other. Tom hollers, "I'll bite your damned nose off ef ya don't give up." Tim made some kind of answer and he hadn't got the words out of his mouth when Tom retched out and did it. Yes sir I didn't think he had enough teeth left in his head but he bit the tip off of Tim's nose. He spat the nose out on the street. After thet Tim was knowed as No Nose Tim er just No Nose. Tim and Tom, when they healed up again, became the best of friends and were partners in the same old saloon.

Source: William E. "Billy the kid" Huntington of Lockwood, Montana. At the time of this interview, Mr. Huntington was seventy-nine years old and had lived in Montana for sixty-five years.
Collector: Chet M. Simpson

SAVING THE BARREL GOODS

A *ccording to old timers, the big Havre fire in 1902 provided the most exciting period in the history of the city.* Although the conflagration was at the time a hard blow to the town's businessmen, it was really instrumental in transforming the city from a huddle of wooden shacks to its present substantial construction of brick and stone.

The fire destroyed all of what is now Havre's main business block, which contains such well-known places as the Havre Hotel and Security Bank. A poor water supply and lack of adequate fire fighting equipment allowed the flames to spread rapidly, and about all the volunteer firemen could do was salvage as much stock as possible from the threatened buildings.

The disaster was not without humorous episodes, and E. G. Miller, who acted as a special fire department officer, recalls the frantic efforts put forth by a saloonkeeper to save his large stock of whiskey. In his basement he had forty barrels of whiskey. The stock was worth a lot of money, and the saloon man ran to the main street as the flames approached his drinking emporium. He carried a roll of bills in his hand and hailed every driver of a vehicle in sight. Passing a five-dollar bill into the hands of each teamster, he directed them to go to the rear of his saloon and load up the spirits from the cellar. Soon a dozen wagons were lined up in rear of the saloon, and each driver hauled away as many barrels as his conveyance would accommodate. The proprietor did not bother to salvage the shelf goods from the saloon, as he felt he had done a mighty good stroke of business in saving the large whiskey stock in barrels. He watched the flames consume his building, and then went home in a peaceful frame of mind.

"We're a mighty lucky couple Mary," he said to his wife. "If I hadn't used my head to good advantage today, we'd be broke now. I saved all my barrel goods, and now I'll get a new location and make money. I've got whiskey enough to last for two years of big business."

"I know you're awfully level-headed in emergencies Jim, and I think it was wonderful of you to think of hiring all those teamsters. By the way, where did they store the whiskey?" asked his wife.

And there was the question that was to set all Havre agog for many days to come. The self-satisfied saloon man had failed to give his teamsters any directions, with the result that they loaded up and pulled out with their freight, free to go in any direction chosen. In other words, the purveyor of hangovers had made each teamster a present of as much liquor as his outfit could haul.

At different points in the city, brawls and drunken rascality shook the tranquility of the town. Hasty responses to urgent calls were made by the police. At one house the officers walked into a kitchen and were shocked to see a red-eyed aggregation of soaks grouped around a whiskey barrel. They weren't using glasses, each man waiting to take his turn at a small rubber hose which protruded from the bunghole of the barrel.

It didn't require any great detective work to locate most of the missing barrels. A policy of watchful waiting was adopted by the police, and one by one the reports of disorderly houses led to the finding of sadly depleted barrels. A few bottles of spirits in the possession of the teamsters would probably not have caused much commotion, but when a man has perhaps six full barrels in his house, and possesses a coterie of thirsty neighbors, the supply is too large to bring about anything but a glorious climax of alcoholized pyrotechnics.

Source: E. G. Miller *was a member of the Havre Fire Brigade at the time of the Havre fire.*
Collector: W. H. Campbell *of Chinook, Montana*

THE BOOTLEGGER

*A*ccording to the police authorities of this area, bootleggers are *exceptionally astute men, and the various ways in which they suc-* ceed in dodging arrest are novel and in some cases downright examples *of genius.* They pinched a man here once after he had successfully sold whiskey in the open for over a year. He took an agency for a certain brand of liniment and shipped in a case. Substituting whiskey for the liniment, he delivered it regularly to his customers for a long period. When caught finally, he claimed that he hadn't done any real harm, as the liniment the company sent him was a fake, and wouldn't cure anything, whereas his booze was never under ninety-proof and could cure anything from snake-bite to extreme melancholia.

Collector: *W. H. Campbell of Chinook, Montana*

BUTTE WAKES

*T*he Irish colony in Butte follows the custom of holding "wakes" or, *in other words, sitting up with the dead.* At these wakes liquor is plentiful and sometimes even the corpse is given a drink. The mourners at one wake, so the story goes, decided to go down to Con People's Saloon after they ran out of liquor. They couldn't leave the corpse alone in the house, so two of the men put the arms of the corpse over their shoulders and carried the dead man along with them. They entered the saloon, propped the corpse against the bar, and then walked to a room in the rear.

The bartender, seeing what he supposed to be a drunk with head hanging over the bar, went over and told the corpse that he'd better be going home. No answer. The bartender spoke again and again. Not getting any response, his anger rose. Grabbing a bung-starter, he hit the corpse over the head and said, "I'll teach yez to answer when yer spoken to."

The corpse fell back on the floor and the bartender was horror-stricken when he saw that the man was dead. He called the friends of the dead man and pointing to him said, "The dirty rat pulled a knife on me and I had to kill 'im."

Source and collector: unknown

A Refreshed Cook

*M*r. E. G. Bright relates an incident that occurred back in 1889 while he was riding for the LX outfit. They were shipping a herd of beef out of Miles City; their camp was about two miles out of town. The boys had just finished loading the cattle, and as usual were proceeding to go up town for some refreshments. Just about dark, the cook from their camp, a little short Scotchman whose name was Alex Fitzgerald, came riding in, and proceeded along with the other boys to have a good time and refresh himself. Some time past midnight when they all decided to go back to camp, Alex didn't seem to be able to mount his saddle horse. So Bright and a couple of the others helped him into the saddle, and as they proceeded on their way, Alex just couldn't balance himself and it was hard for the others to keep him from falling off his horse. Then they decided to play a little trick on him. Soon they came past the graveyard. Here they stopped and placed Alex over inside the fence, leaving him in safety where nothing could run over or hurt him, and they continued on to camp. The next morning when their boss, Jim Drummond, went to call the cook, there was no cook there. So Jim inquired of the boys if they knew where Alex was, and they informed him that they had left Alex a short distance up the road.

Jim requested someone go get him so they might have breakfast. Bright and a couple of the others started out, upon reaching the spot where Alex was sleeping they called to him. "Hey Alex, it's time to get up, we want breakfast." Upon awakening he raised up, rubbed his eyes, stretched himself, looked all about him and said, "Aha! resurrection day, and I'm the first Son of a B—— up."

Source: E. G. Bright of Terry, Montana. At the time of this interview, Mr. Bright had been a cowpuncher and rancher in Prairie County for fifty-five years.
Collector: Fred Like

The Hunter and the Mule

*T*he story of the hunter and the mule is becoming a legend in Montana. It is often related in Livingston and is told and retold during the elk-hunting season. It is a favorite in barbershops, and whenever it is told there is sure to be an argument over the "true" facts of the incident. The general trend of the story is that a hunter who had tipped the bottle too often went up into the region around Gardiner to shoot an elk. He saw what he thought was an elk in the brush, shot and killed it, only to discover he had killed a mule. Some say the hunter did not discover his mistake until he had dressed the animal and loaded it into his car. Only then did he discover it was a mule because it had shoes on. Some say the hunter was a "feller from Philadelphia or New York," or some other eastern city. Others state he was a rancher and that he shot his own mule and was about to cook some of the meat when he discovered his mistake.

Another version of the tale has it that the mule was owned by an old lady and that she had the hunter arrested and there is a record of his paying a fine. Just where this record can be found is never revealed. The variations of the hunter and the mule story are almost infinite. The one point upon which all who tell it seem to agree is that the hunter was exceedingly drunk. Some say that the hunter brought the mule into Livingston and sold the meat to local restaurants. No one can predict what astounding embellishments this story will gather in future years.

Collector: Elmer Baird of Roundup, Montana

CROSS-EYED PETE AND THE GRAVEDIGGER

There was an old Indian scout and prospector that hung around the saloons of Billings in the early days that was cross-eyed but a crackerjack shot with the sixgun. They'd make all kinds of fun of old Cross-eyed Pete by asking, "Which eye is lookin' at me, Pete?" Pete would take it all good naturedly and laugh, too.

One fellow in particular picked on Pete. That was the gravedigger of Boothill. He had buried so many leftovers from gun brawls and drunken gun fights that the dead didn't unnerve him any. The gravedigger had his eye set on a huge diamond ring which Cross-eyed Pete wore on his right little finger. If there was anything Pete liked to show, it was that big diamond. He'd blow his breath on it and shine it up on his shirtfront. Even when he was very drunk he'd stop and shine her up.

The gravedigger would drink with Peter just to get a good look at the ring and admire its brilliance. The two would rib each other constantly and were good pals. The gravedigger would say, "Well, when you're dead, Pete, I'll take that diamond off your rotten carcass." The gravedigger was reported to not be above stealing from the dead.

Cross-eyed Pete would answer, "Like hell you will, you dirty grave robber. If you do, I'll haunt ya, so help me, I'll haunt ya to your dying day." They'd laugh and slap each other on the back and buy more drinks.

Well, to cap the climax old Pete did get mighty sick and lay dying on his bunk. The gravedigger could hardly wait fer the day. One morning the local sawbones came to look old Cross-eye over and had to pronounce him dead. They fixed up a coffin out of old pine boards and buried old Pete.

Sure enough the gravedigger slipped back the first night and dug up the grave. There was that sparklin' diamond—the very thing he'd been wanting and waiting fer for years. He tried and tried to get it off old dead Pete's little finger. No go. The ring wouldn't budge. It had been on that finger so long that flesh had grown up on each side of the ring and it was embedded. In desperation the gravedigger fetched out his Bowie knife and cut off the finger. He gleefully put on the ring although trembling for the first time in years.

Well sar, when he cut off that finger and the blood started running it must have caused old Cross-eyed Pete to come alive. Anyway he raised up and looked at the gravedigger wearing his diamond. The sight caused him to grow to a white-hot anger. He climbed out of the grave madder than a hornet and took out after the gravedigger.

The gravedigger was so scared and surprised that he couldn't get his legs to do what he wanted them to do, and before he knew it he had stumbled over a tombstone. Pete came up breathing hard and said, "Gimme back my diamond, you dirty rat." The gravedigger gladly returned the diamond and begged, "Don't kill me, Pete, don't kill me for God's sakes. I'll never do it again, Pete. I didn't know you could haunt like that."

Cross-eyed Pete lived for two years more but that gravedigger never was the same man, and it sure broke him from robbing the dead. I think it was a case of the sawbones thinking the man was dead when the fellow was really still alive.

*Source: Herbert A. "Herb" Roberts of Billings, Montana. At the time of this inter-
view, Mr. Roberts was seventy-three years old and retired. After telling the above
story of Cross-eyed Pete, Mr. Roberts went on in detail about several cases he knew
of where people were buried alive in the old days: "Doctors were well named horse
doctors then. Once in a while you'd run onto a damned good one, though."
Collector: Chet M. Simpson*

BEER RUSTLING

I've *heard this story of the printers of the old* Butte Intermountain *tapping the beer lines so often that I suppose it might be classified
as folklore.*

The pressroom of the *Butte Intermountain* in Butte's early days was in the basement of their building on Main Street. Next door was the basement of a saloon where the beer kegs were placed. Because of the situation the beer lines had to run across the ceiling of one corner of the composing room. One day a printer discovered that the pipes contained beer. A hand drill was obtained, a hole was bored and plugged with a dutchman. From then on the printers rustled their own beer cost free. The bartenders noticed that their kegs ran short and investigated but the dutchman was pretty well camouflaged and went unnoticed. They didn't care to press the investigation too closely for that if the printers hadn't discovered the beer lines it would give them ideas. Just after the Butte-Anaconda Printers' mulligan, an affair that lasted several days, the boys had dry throats. They began hitting the dutchman pretty heavily and soon they were laid out in various degrees of drunkenness. One printer finally either forgot to replace the dutchman or didn't plug it in tight and the beer leaked onto the floor. Soon the kegs ran dry and an investigation showed where the beer had been going.

Source: Charles Hardy of Missoula, Montana. At the time of this interview, Mr. Hardy was an instructor of typography at the School of Journalism, Montana State University. He had been in Montana since 1908 and had, at different times, lived in Miles City, Forsyth, Butte, Anaconda, and Missoula.
Collector: Edward B. Reynolds of Missoula, Montana. On his interview form, Mr. Reynolds noted that he had heard an addition to Mr. Hardy's above-related story: "Prior to the discovery [of the tapped beer lines], the owner of the saloon was chosen county commissioner of Silver Bow County. The printers entertained him at a beer bust. He in turn reciprocated with a party of his own. Later . . . he discovered that he had been treated with his own beer."

PRE-PAID CELEBRATION

O n November 21, 1889, one of Butte's judges received the surprise of his life when John Dough walked into police court and nonchalantly and soberly informed his honor that he intended to get drunk and disorderly. He said he was determined to become inebriated for a day and desired to have his trial pronto and pay whatever fines the judge wished to impose. The charges amounted to eleven dollars, one dollar, and costs, which Mr. Dough willingly paid. Upon being paid the judge told the man he could go and perform as he intended.

"Thanks, Judge," replied the potential celebrant. "Does that mean biling drunk?"

"Yes, drunk as a boiled owl."

"Does it include disorderly conduct?"

"Everything."

"Thanks," he said and walked out.

Collector: Edward J. Connors collected this story from the Anaconda Standard *of November 22, 1889.*

TALES OF TRUE WESTERNERS

*Crown Prince Olav and Crown
Princess Martha of Norway at
Two Medicine Chalet in Glacier
National Park with Rising
Wolf Mountain in the background. The royal couple
proudly wear western riding
outfits and their horses sport a
silver mounted saddle and
bridle—all gifts presented to
them at their official welcoming
in Helena, Montana.*

Photo by Byerly (#249)

LIVER-EATING JOHNSON'S TWO JACKS AND TWO EIGHTS

I'll tell you about my first meeting Liver-eating Johnson. It was about the second winter I spent out here in Montana and one day I rode into Coulson. Coulson was the first settlement anywhere near the now-present site of Billings. It was a steamboat landing near where the east bridge is at present. The steamboat *Josephine* came up the Yellowstone River this far to unload supplies.

There was a hurdy-gurdy in Coulson where you could gamble or drink whiskey over the bar. All you had to have in those days to start a saloon or hurdy-gurdy was a barrel of whiskey and a big pine plank for a bar. This owner and bartender could mix fancy drinks if you desired. Most of the boys said that if you got a skinful of these drinks and a rattlesnake bit you, it would kill the rattlesnake. Another common reference to the power of this old-time whiskey was that it would make a jackrabbit spit in a rattle-snake's eye.

As I was saying I rode into town one bitterly cold day. I tied my horse out in front of the hurdy-gurdy and then went inside. It was a poor day for business. Some big rawboned fellow was there in buckskins. I was told it was Liver-eating Johnson. I had heard a lot about this fellow since I'd been out in Montana. How he pretended to eat an Indian's liver in front of other Indians. The Indians thought he did because he had the liver on the end of his knife and put the stuff to his mouth. He did this to scare the Indians and I was told they sure feared him.

Anyhow, old scout Liver-eating Johnson was there in the hurdy-gurdy besides a tramp and the bartender owner. I gathered that some good natured kidding was going on between the bartender and Johnson before I got here. Johnson was a big man and well muscled and so was the bartender. I think the barkeep thought he could whip old Liver-eating. The barkeep kept hollering, "Why don't you buy a drink? Why don't you buy a drink?"

When I came in I shook off the snow and took my big buffalo hide overcoat off. That was a prize possession in those days. I went over by the big stove to get warm. While I was warming up I noticed Johnson's rifle leaning against the wall. I noticed that Johnson or the bartender neither wore guns. I heard the ribbing was still going on and so I thought I'd buy everybody a drink and which I did. This drink served to warm me up quicker. I was nearly chilled through.

The barkeep suggested we try our luck at stud poker since there wasn't much else to do. Johnson and I had to stake the tramp to some chips. That was the way it was in those days. Everybody was free-hearted and friendly and if a man didn't have anything, people thought nothing of staking him. Well, in the poker game the barkeep and Johnson were still razzing each other. The barkeep had a fancy vest. In the old days a man wore his vest as much as his shirt. The vests were gaudy affairs.

This barkeeper had such a gaudy vest. Liver-eating Johnson drew a winning hand of two jacks and two eights and as he was raking in the chips that he won, the bartender popped off, "Aha!" He sez, "You got the death hand, Johnson. You're gong to die pretty soon. That's the hand that killed Wild Bill." This was pretty rough kidding to say the least. In a flash Johnson came to life. He reached across the poker table and grabbed the bartender with his left hand. With his right fist he bounced on the chin of the unsuspecting bartender. It all happened so suddenly that I hardly got to see all of it.

I'm telling you when the barkeep came to, he was a pretty decent hombre after that. The two jacks and two eights that he was referring to was the very hand that Wild Bill Hickok held when he was shot in the back. That was on everybody's mind then, because it wasn't long before Wild Bill had been killed. It was known all through the West as the death hand and it was fightin' words to mention it.

It was a peculiar incident that I should meet up with Liver-eating Johnson and hear about the death hand of poker all in the same day. Well, it was common knowledge afterwards that it had no effect on Johnson's death for he didn't die until long after this incident. Liver-eating Johnson was a great scout of the west and a mighty swell guy to meet.

Source: George L. Danford of Billings, Montana. At the time of this interview, Mr. Danford was eighty-four years old, had lived in Montana for sixty-two years, and owned an irrigated farm on the Billings-Laurel road.
Collector: Chet M. Simpson

Roosevelt and I Hunted for Goats

*J*ohn Willis, *famous for his long association with President Theodore Roosevelt as guide and companion on his hunting trips into the Rockies, arrived in Montana from Missouri, along with his brother, the late C. C. Willis, following the advent of the Northern Pacific Railroad.* He maintained his headquarters in Thompson Falls, operating pack trains into the mining districts of the Coeur d'Alene country and serving as guide for the big game hunters.

In 1886 Willis received a letter from New York, the gist of which was: "I have heard that you act as a guide for hunting parties out in Montana and are familiar with the mountains on which range the famous Rocky Mountain goats. I am anxious to obtain one of these animals. Do you suppose if I came out there that I could shoot one of them?"

The letter was signed "Theodore Roosevelt," then, of course, not as famous or as well-known as he later came to be upon his accession to the Presidency of the United States. To Willis he was but another of those Eastern tenderfeet who wished to engage his services as a guide.

The handwriting was not any too legible and Willis, after finally deciphering the contents, turned the letter over and scribbled on the back of it words somewhat like the following: "No, I do not believe that you could shoot a goat—that is, unless you can shoot a darned sight better than you can write."

Shortly thereafter Willis received a wire that Roosevelt would reach Thompson Falls on a certain day. When the train arrived two men alighted and approached Willis, who was waiting on the platform. One was a strapping specimen of manhood, fitted out in true Western style, looking fit for anything from riding a bucking bronco to scaling the highest peak in the Rockies with a fifty-pound knapsack on his back.

His companion, as Willis later told him, looked like a rich

brewer's son from New England. Of stocky build, but with pink cheeks, prominent teeth, thick-lensed glasses and, of all things, wearing a pair of plus fours or knickerbockers. The latter especially irked Willis. He looked like anything but a big-game hunter and when he approached Willis and introduced himself as Theodore Roosevelt you could have knocked off the latter's bulging eyes with a switch. His companion, who Willis thought must be Roosevelt, was introduced as Roosevelt's ranch manager on his North Dakota ranch.

The knee breeches were still sour to Willis and he told Roosevelt he didn't think the latter could carry a heavy pack and rifle and still scale the heights where the mountain goats had their habitat. "Well, you just wait and see," said Teddy, as they went to Willis' headquarters to get their outfit together.

They started out for the Bitterroot Mountains and made camp on the banks of a stream in the valley. Then they began the long hikes up the peaks in search of the elusive goat. Roosevelt proved that he could take it, for he packed his load and stood the arduous climbing as well as either of his companions. Within a short time he got his chance at a goat and wounded the animal, which made off to the higher crags with Teddy on its trail. Once he fell about fifty feet into a gully, but, undaunted although considerably bruised and shaken, this indomitable man was up and after his quarry. He succeeded in getting a fine specimen to take back to New York. He stood his share of camp duties without a murmur and altogether had a bully time.

By this time Willis was his fast friend and admirer and the two remained loyal friends and occasional hunting companions even after Roosevelt became President. On the occasion of the President's visit to Helena, his first inquiry on alighting from the train was for Jack Willis, "the long Missourian," as he called him. Jack, of course, was on hand, trying to be inconspicuous among the many politicians, but Roosevelt spotted him and insisted that he ride with him in the parade through the streets of Helena to the capitol.

Willis refused all remuneration for his services as guide on this first hunting trip and Roosevelt and his ranch manager were welcome guests at the Willis home while in Thompson Falls. Just as the train was leaving on its return to New York Roosevelt reached out to shake hands with Willis and when the latter opened his hand he found a package of bills amounting to something like $500 or $600. Willis was as mad as a hatter, but there was nothing he could do about it just then, for the train was on its way, with the grinning "brewer's son" waving at him.

Willis decided to send the money back to New York, but didn't know Roosevelt's address, for Teddy was not the prominent personage at that time which he later became. So Willis decided to write to New York to find out the proper address before sending the money. Soon came a letter back from Roosevelt with words to this effect: "Don't be a fool. I sold an article describing my experiences on my trip out there to a magazine for around $1,300. As my expenses amounted to about $700, and I gave you $600, nobody lost anything and we are all square, besides having a wonderful time."

Willis, who is still living in California and occasionally makes a visit to his relatives in Plains, attended Roosevelt's inauguration ceremonies in Washington, D.C., when the latter was elected President in 1908.

He was urged many times by the President to be a guest at the White House, but steadfastly declined because, as he intimated many times, "nobody could ever get him into one of those dad-fangled dress suits."

Source: Griffith A. Williams of Plains, Montana

KID ROYAL

*S*heriff Oscar Fallang was bringing "Kid Royal" back from Deer Lodge
to testify in the trial of his horse-thief partner, Arthur Charlesworth,
and help clean up the epidemic of rustling that had beset Sweet Grass
County ranches for several years.

The Kid had volunteered to testify in the Charlesworth case, so
it had seemed perfectly safe to permit the Kid to go alone to the
washroom. Safe, that is, until Sheriff Fallang aroused himself with
the realization that the Kid had been gone far longer than was
necessary.

Kid Royal had been notorious in southern Montana for most of
two decades. He had been Sheriff Fallang's chief headache during
much of his four terms in office.

Best known by his nickname, Kid Royal had been born Mike
Hall, but during a greater part of his adult life he had been just a
number behind the massive walls at Deer Lodge. He went to prison
for three years for horse theft in 1890 in Livingston. Two subsequent
convictions had kept him out of circulation a good part of the time,
with intervals of freedom in between his tangles with the law. He
had served two years of a ten-year stretch when he started back to
Big Timber for the trial of his partner.

It was near Bozeman that the Kid went to the water cooler. He
entered the washroom and locked the door. Then he broke out a
window, swung down the side of the coach, holding by his
manacled hands, and dropped to the right of way.

Fallang offered a reward of $500 for the Kid's capture, but the
hide-and-seek game that started beside the railroad track continued for almost a year.

The Kid wasn't lazy. He was a good ranch hand when he
wanted to be. He got a job herding sheep through the winter in
Meagher County. But when spring came the Kid appropriated a
horse, saddle and rifle and started back toward Sweet Grass

County. His new mount turned out to be an outlaw. At the first opportunity, the Kid caught up a couple of mares and turned the outlaw loose. Then at the Charles Geary ranch in the Shields Valley he added a big black saddle horse to his string.

At the Lovely ranch near Clyde Park he added a couple of fine Clydesdale mares to his growing herd. He turned back north through the Potter basin and picked up three sets of harness, down Sixteen-Mile Creek to the Missouri River and up to Toston, where he added Tom Hudson's wagon to his assets.

From circulars that had been broadcast, Sheriff Dedmond of Broadwater County recognized the Kid and arrested him not far from Whitehall. The Kid was headed for Idaho. He had property from ranches in five southern Montana counties, including a feather bed and three feather pillows.

The Kid was brought back to Big Timber to face the music. Since the stolen property was no longer of value to him, the Kid drew a map, indicating the ranches he had visited and the property was returned to its owners.

"There are half a dozen fine mares at the Adams ranch at Melville. When I get out I'm going to get those mares," the Kid told Fallang while he awaited his hearing in Big Timber.

One June day shortly before the Kid was to plead guilty in district court, Undersheriff Dell Whitney released the prisoners into the jail corridor to clean it up. After making sure all the locks were in order, Whitney went up town for a shave. When he returned an hour later the bars in the transom between the jail and the office had been spread. The Kid, a small fellow in his middle thirties, was gone!

Late that day a horse was stolen from Henry Rowland's ranch while it was tied near a blacksmith shop. At the John Lovelace ranch in the Shields Valley another horse was stolen. The Kid spent a night at the John Morris ranch on Little Timber Creek south of the Crazy Mountains. Charles Shook, employed by Mr. Morris, was an old acquaintance of the Kid, and said he was going to Big Timber for the county fair.

"I might go down and take in that fair myself," the Kid replied.

After he was gone, the Morris family got word to the Park and Sweet Grass County officers who set posses on the trail.

At the Adams ranch at Melville the Kid took those fine mares he had boasted about to Sheriff Fallang. Trailing north through Fergus County and into the Gallatin Valley, he reached an unoccupied ranch near Twin Bridges and turned out his string of eight horses into the pasture. Apparently warned that he was being trailed, the Kid disappeared. The officers appeared close behind the Kid, and though they watched at night for a week, the Kid did not return.

Sheriff Ed Reynolds of Gallatin County captured the Kid at Manhattan after a rancher there had recognized him.

Back in Big Timber again, the Kid pleaded guilty to his latest crimes and begged the court for leniency.

"I want to buy books and study while I am in prison this time," he said. "I want to get ready for a better life and honest work when I get out."

"You will have ample time for study in prison," he was informed by the late Judge Frank Henry. "Your sentence for the crime of which you stand guilty will be fourteen years."

This, added to the eight years of the old sentence, made a total of twenty-two years ahead.

The Kid, it is recorded, had plenty of "sand." He did not know fear. But in all his owl-hooting he never carried a gun.

"I have found out," he said, "that a man can get into enough trouble without carrying a gun to get him into more."

Source: *Douglas Goosey of Big Timber, Montana. Mr. Goosey reported that his references for the story were the* Sweet Grass News *and Mrs. O. Fallang.*

KID CURRY MEETS BROTHER VAN

Years ago, when Kid Curry and his gang held up the Great Northern train at Exeter Siding, four miles west of Malta, there was one passenger who left the scene a richer man.

On the train was W. A. Van Orsdel, an old-time Methodist preacher known to all and sundry as Brother Van. He viewed with interest the businesslike manner in which the collection was taken up by Curry as, hat in one hand and six-gun in the other, the outlaw sauntered down the aisle. At last the Kid shoved his hat in front of Brother Van for the latter to "shell out."

The preacher complied with the request but the result was discouraging. Curry looked puzzled at the loose change that clinked into the hat and inquired, "How come?" A man traveling on the railroad would naturally have more money than that.

"I'm a preacher," explained Brother Van.

"You are?" exclaimed Curry, beginning to understand. "What kind of a preacher?"

"I'm a Methodist."

A twinkle appeared in the eye of the famous outlaw. "I'm sort of a Methodist myself," he grinned as he handed Brother Van a five-dollar bill.

Collector: Guy H. Rader

POKES, PUNCHERS, HERDERS, THE RANGE, AND THEIR CRITTERS

TEETH FOR TWO

There was an old couple that owned a ranch on Poverty Flats near Edgar, Montana. The old gentleman had fought Indians and was one of the first settlers in that part of Montana. The reason I'm telling this story is that I ran into one of the worst cases of tightwads I believe in my life. I never believed that anybody could be that saving and economical.

I was just a young buck at the time and had only been out in this country for a short time. I was looking for work and any kind of work since I only had about two or three dollars to my name. Somebody referred me to this old couple and I asked for a job. I got it.

They had a small batch of alfalfa hay to put up. It was my duty to mow, rake, and bunch the hay. While I was working there, I noticed at every meal that the old man ate his meal with me, but I never did see the old lady eat. I never gave it much thought. I was too tired from the long hours I put in and the hard work to ponder on whether the old lady was off her feed or not. I figured she either ate her meal before or after I got to the house. It was no business of mine.

A lapse of memory on my part soon solved the mystery. One noon after a meal I left without taking my gloves. I had forgotten them. I had the horses hitched up to the rake before I realized that I didn't have my gloves. My gloves I *must* have. My hands were quite tender—so nothing to do but stop at the house on the way out to the field and get my gloves.

I never took the precaution of tying the horses up for I meant to dash into the house and out again. I ran to the door and walked briskly into the house. There I found the reason for the odd action of only the old man eating at mealtime. The old lady had a set of false teeth in the basin and was in the act of washing them. It seems that the old man had taken them out of his head after he had eaten his meal and now she was going to use them to eat with. That she did—every meal.

After the secret was out they didn't make any bones about it. She used to nag him about leaving bits of chewing tobacco on the teeth. I stayed on all winter and did the chores for board and keep. I slept in the kitchen on an old cot. They slept in the bedroom—the other half of the crude log cabin.

She had the teeth last in the evening and would put them in a glass of water before going to bed. One very cold morning we were all awakened abruptly by a rapid tapping or rapping. The noise came from the table and would you believe it, those teeth were chattering like a machine gun. You couldn't blame them because the water was partially frozen. I grabbed the glass and poured the teeth on the table. They chattered, twittered, and fluttered around on top of the table. I got a heavy army blanket and put it around them, and they stopped shivering. Just before I got back into the cot, I heard them say from under the blanket, "Thanks, Kid!" That's s' fact.

Source: Ralph L. Simpson of Billings, Montana. At the time of this interview, Mr. Simpson was sixty-five years old and had owned a ranch on Cold Creek of the Shane Ridge plateau between Joliet and Columbus, Montana.
Collector: Chet M. Simpson

THE CHAPS TREATMENT

*I*n the old days there was always somebody jobbing somebody. The boys would travel in bunches from one saloon to the other. The least excuse was used to pull off a good one on some unsuspecting guy. One rancher I remember distinctly who was used as a butt of many a joke.

He'd come into town, tie his horse up at the hitching pole, and be drunk for weeks. The poor pony would patiently stand there without being watered or fed. Some of the boys generally took the pony to the livery stable and saw to it that it was watered and fed. They got tired of helping him out this way and besides, the guy was a nuisance.

The leader of the bunch decided to hunt out the drunken rancher and fix him up good. Teach him a lesson so that he wouldn't want to get drunk again for a long time.

They found him in one of the saloons so tipsy he didn't know much what he was doing. The boys dressed him up in old squaw clothes, braided his hair in two long braids, put big turkey feathers in his hair, got a blanket and put it around him, and painted his face hideously with vermillion or war paint. They even went so far as to strap a big wooden doll on his back for a papoose.

After the boys had paraded him through town and got a lot of laughs out of it, they put him on his horse and sent him home. Of course the horse got him home all right, for the drunk didn't know which way was what. His cowpokes got a big kick out of it and when he sobered up, he was fighting mad. He said he'd get even with that bunch in town that did it. He proceeded to strap two guns on and come into town shootin'.

One of his own cowpokes saw this would never do, so he slipped into town ahead of the mad rancher. When the angry rancher entered town, everybody was waiting for him. Two of the boys roped him off his horse as he entered the outskirts for they were hid in some willows along the road. This way they got his guns away from him and made him walk on into town with the lassoes around his arms held tight to his body.

Everybody met him as he came to town and then grabbed arms and legs and carried him horizontally into a saloon that had a pool table. They laid him belly-down on the pool table and somebody took off his leather chaps and gave the sorehead the chaps treatment. Everybody'd take a crack with the chaps across the buttocks of this poor sport rancher. If he was still mad, they'd make him buy the drinks for the crowd.

You had to know how to take it or the boys would make it very miserable for a pouter. That's the way the West was in those days. If you needed money or got some tough luck somehow or other, these very pranksters would give you the shirt off their back or the last dollar they had.

Source: Herbert A. "Herb" Roberts of Billings, Montana. At the time of this interview, Mr. Roberts was seventy-three years old, retired, and was known as an old-time prankster.
Collector: Chet M. Simpson

FIREBUGS

I was the instigator once of grazing cow critters at night and makin'
two-year-olds out of one-year-olds in half the time.

It was a great scheme. I'd learned from an Indian the secret of finding the firebug nests. This Indian swore me not to tell and I couldn't reveal only on penalty of death. About all I can say is that there are certain trees that these bugs take to and live under the loose bark. There's a special way of getting to them.

I'd almost forgotten this trick I'd been taught by the Indian. I got a handful of these firebugs fer fun one night while ridin' night-hawk. One steer wouldn't lie down with the rest of the herd and kept making a dash fer a creek nearby. I'd have to bring him galloping back. It was getting black as pitch and storm clouds were hanging low. Well, I went and got these firebugs and I could see my horse and saddle plain from the soft glow of light put out by the bugs.

Mr. Steer took another plunge fer the creek. I went over and dabbed my rope on him or where I thought he was and sure enough I got him. I spilled him good and hard to knock the wind out of the ornery critter. While he was getting his wind, I got off my horse and came over to look at him. He looked bug-eyed at me a-showin' them firebugs. Then I got an idea. Why not use them bugs to keep track of him? I was chewin' a big wad of pine gum. I daubed this pine gum on the brand D-Z and stuck the firebugs into the gum. It sure showed up plain, and to make it good I stuck a firebug on the tip of each horn. Then I let him up.

Mr. Steer raced off as if to run away from that soft glow of light. He seed he couldn't shake that off and then I tailed him so close he give up the idea of going fer the creek again. It sure worked miracles. You could locate that critter anywhere in the herd. He couldn't help from noticing the grass he e-luminated and so he started to graze like he would in the daytime.

The other nighthawkers wanted to know what set that critter on fire. I told 'em it wasn't fire but firebugs. They had to all go over and see fer themselves. When we were watching the steer he had already by then learned to twist his rump with the brand side toward his head. This flashed the full glow of that firebug-studded D-Z. He could see almost as clear as day.

The boss got wind of it and thought it was such a good idea that he insisted we fix the whole herd like that. We did just that. It took about two barrels of firebugs and a barrel of molasses for it was too hard to chew and find pine gum. The whole herd was lit up like a church—calves and all. It sure was a pretty sight. Them firebugs a-winkin' and blinkin' at different intervals. We even put firebugs on the teets of the breed cows so the calves could plainly see where their night lunch was located and could find their right mammy.

You could practically hear the meat piling on them beef. All good things, I guess, come to bad, for them breed cows were givin' so much milk that the calves were bloated like ticks and were actually floundered on milk. Then one old bossy sprung a leak in an udder. I guess you might say an udder leak. The noise was "Pssst-shush." Finally there was udder leaks springing all over the place and milk squirting in the critters' eyes.

They stampeded. Boy! Whata stampede. It happened at night and it looked like a streak of fire a skimming across the prairie. They ran and ran, and trampled a number of their own critters. The heat of their bodies melted the molasses and the firebugs fell to the ground to be trampled to death. I had to skip the country fer I's to blame fer all that mess. First I was a wizard and then I's made a bum all over night.

Source: William E. "Billy the Kid" Huntington of Lockwood, Montana. At the time of this interview, Mr. Huntington was seventy-nine years old and had lived in Montana for sixty-five years.
Collector: Chet M. Simpson

POWERFUL MONTANA ECHO

*D*uring *the cattle days in Montana we used to have an assorted collection of cowboys.* All of 'em were pretty good singers and it is about this singin' habit that I'm a-headin' to a point in my story.

I remember one feller in particular. I guess I'll never forget him and how he got shed of the singin' habit. I can still laugh myself silly now when I think about it.

I had him hired to herd a string of beef I had. Right off the bat I couldn't help noticin' his fancy riggin' on his saddle and chaps. Silver conchas on his horse's bridle and silver inlay work on his saddle. Then I noticed him the first day a-lookin' at his shadow or a-gazin' at his picture in the river as he let his horse get a drink of water. He had to have his hat just so and neckerchief this way. He was what we called a pretty cowboy.

I began to think he wasn't worth his salt but he proved me wrong there. He sure knew how to rope 'n' brand 'n' all of that. But his biggest feature was his singin'. He knew more damned songs—Irish songs and otherwise. The one he overdid was "Buffalo Gal" and did I get sick and tired of hearin' it.

One day he was singin' until hell-wouldn't-have-it and we was drivin' some stranded cows out of a box canyon. It was a peculiar canyon and about all I can say about it was that it looked kinda haunted and desolate. I couldn't figure why the cattle wandered up into it because there wasn't much grass there.

As the cowboy sang we began to notice an increasingly loud echo. The echo finally out-drowned the cowboy. He laughed at this and the laugh came back at us in a hideous manner and kinda shook us in the saddle. The cowboy couldn't leave well enough alone. He knew it wasn't safe to sing, so not giving up he started to hum a ditty. Boy! That ditty came back magnified a hundredfold for it came upon us a-screamin' and knocked the cowboy completely out of the saddle and tore the shirt off my back. The cowboy's horse was even jostled up a little.

The cowboy got up and got on his horse again but he didn't let out a whisper. You couldn't. That certain spot was bad for an echo to shove the airwaves around. You may not believe that, but that's what actually happened. I was fit to be tied for wantin' to laugh but I didn't dare and it shore broke that cowboy from singin'. He didn't sing in canyons after that. Oh, of course he sang out on the prairie.

Source: E. L. "Dick" Grewell. At the time of this interview, Mr. Grewell was seventy-one years old and had lived in Montana for fifty-two years.
Collector: Chet M. Simpson

Mother Nature Helps

*A*n unusual situation developed one year when I and a cowboy swam some cattle across the Clarks Fork. We got the cattle across the river all right except four calves who landed on a small half-moon shaped shoal near a steep bank. There was no way to drive the calves off the shoal because the steep bank ran abruptly to an end in the swift current of the river. The only way I could see offhand to rescue them was to swim your horse again in the river and run them off the shoal into the river until they arrived at a river-high bank.

The cowboy that was with me saw that I was worried and he says, "What are ya worried about? Them calves are as easy as pie to get up on that bank."

I says, "I don't see how unless you go into that river again."

He laughed and offered me a chaw of his Climax. I took a chaw but it didn't calm me much. The cowboys says, "See that big box elder a-growin' out of that bank? Mother Nachure planted that there fer a purpose. Then she grew a big limb out over the river on that there tree. It's all as plain as day."

I says, "I don't see what you mean pardner. It's as clear as mud to me. And why bring Mother Nachure into this?"

He says, "Holy sassafras! Cain't ya realize what ya got a rope on your saddle fer? I'm tellin' ya, it's made to order." Well, the light began to dawn on me when he mentioned rope. I could visualize what could be done. "Yes siree," says the cowboy. "Ya gotta enlist Mother Nachure as often as ya can because she's mighty helpful if ya can only see her pint of view."

You know that gazaybo dabbed his rope over that limb and gave me instructions to stand on the edge of that bank and rope the calves around the bellies. All of this I did and, he on the other end of the rope with his horse pulled each calf up over the bank. I'd swing the little fellers over onto the bank proper and the cowboy'd let loose of his end of the rope. The calf would plop down hard and have about all his wind knocked out of him. By the time he got his wind back I had the rope off from around his belly and he'd scramble to his feet and skip over and join the rest of the herd.

We did that to all four calves and pretty soon they were all safe and sound. There was nothin' to it and it was just like shootin' fish. But that Mother Nachure angle was a new wrinkle on me. After that when I got myself in a hole out on the range I never forgot to harness Mother Nachure's natural surroundings in figgering my way out of a tough spot.

Source: E. L. *"Dick" Grewell of Billings, Montana. At the time of this interview, Mr. Grewell was seventy-one years old and had lived in Montana for fifty-two years.* **Collector:** *Chet M. Simpson*

TOUGH GUY

There was an extra-ordinary tough guy around Poverty Flats one year that really pulled off a tough demonstration.

It was during the time that men started shavin' and people came to know that a barber existed. The men were slow to take to a smooth face because they considered it sissy to not have a beard.

Well, this tough cowpuncher was always tryin' to show how tough he was whenever the opportunity presented himself and he never lost a chance to do so. He came into the barber shop one day and ordered a shave. Now I was in the barber shop at the time and I saw the whole thing. And believe me, seein' is believin'.

It seems this tough cowpuncher had been complainin' about not having hot towels on his face before the barber shaved him. He made some remark about this subject before he got into the chair. In those days the barber shops usually had a tub full of hot water a-boilin' on a pot bellied stove.

This certain day the water was really steamin' and the towels were playin' tag with each other in that piping hot water. The barber had to reach into this hot inferno with asbestos gloves and then put the steamin' towel on the tough guy's face. He draped the molten hot towel around the puncher's face and it musta parboiled his jaws. I don't see how it could help it.

Anyway, that puncher riz up out of that chair and jerked the towel off his face and he was madder than a pestered hornet. He threw the hot towel still smokin' clear across the barber shop and said, "Sam! (That was the barber's name.) I thought I told you I wanted a hot towel."

Source: E. L. "Dick" Grewell of Billings, Montana. At the time of this interview, Mr. Grewell was seventy-one years old and had lived in Montana for fifty-two years. Collector: Chet M. Simpson

COWS VERSUS KAOUWS

The radio in the corner had been blasting away uninterruptedly for over an hour. The usual afternoon array of blah had been coming in over the long-suffering airways. Program after program—stuffed shirt politicians, the adventures of Ma Jenkins, and so on—played on ad infinitum. No one had been particularly interested. Now it was a cowboy tenor in tremulous tones proclaiming, with the assistance of a so-called hillbilly band, that he was a "Lone-Lonesome Kaouw boy."

Curly Monaghan who knew his cows, and who had been more or less associated with the beasts since his diaper days, strode over the radio disgustedly and with a click of the switch put the lonesome "kaouw boy" out of his misery for that afternoon, at least. "If there's any sort of a critter that burns me up," snorted the aroused Curly as he regained his seat, "It's a so-called cowboy tenor, and any time you hear a blankety blank hoosier call a cow a kaouw I'll show you a blankety son of a blank that never was any closer to a cow than a bald-headed coconut."

It usually was indicative of an informative half hour or so when Curly was sufficiently aroused to pour forth such a tirade on any particular subject. We listened.

"Kaouw," muttered Curly. "Hoosier dialect—Oakie talk— Gimme that dictionary!"

He flipped the pages determinedly. "Webster wrote this long before anyone ever heard of Oakie crooners," he said. "Here it is, as plain as the hair on that would-be singer's pants. Cow—pronounced K—O—U to rhyme with how or sow—and it means the mature female of domestic cattle. And here's cowboy right below it pronounced the same way, which means a bold, dashing, fearless rider employed by a stockman. That's what Webster says."

He closed the book with a bang. "I don't know so much about the bold and dashing and fearless, but I do know any self-respecting cow poke knows better than to call himself a kaouw boy."

Curly was far from finished on the subject. Our smiles only added fuel to his fire, and he continued, "If Webster wanted a cow called a kaouw, don't you suppose he'd have spelled it K-a-o-u-w and make it rhyme with the meouw of a cat. I've punched cows and I've bought and sold cows from one end of Montana to the other," he continued, "from the Canadian border to the Mexican line, and any time I hear a scissorbill say ' kaouw,' I hide my wallet, as poor as it is, and my pride with it. Any honest cowboy who spent any time on the range or on a cattle ranch calls a cow as God named it, C-O-W. And another thing—don't ever leave your wife layin' around loose when there's one of the kaouw men within twenty miles distance. They're a darn sight handier handin' out sweet words that goes to a woman's head, than they are at pokin' cows—C-O-W-S, I mean."

"Where did the ' kaouw' expression originate?" one of the listeners interrupted. It was worth a slight interruption to keep Curly on the subject.

"I'll tell you where it came from," hotly answered Curly. "It came from Texas, that's where it came from. Those Vaqueros, or whatever the hell they call them, brought that twang with them when they herded the first Longhorn north to fatten its starved belly up in God's country. It must've been kaouws they brought with them. God knows, they didn't look like cows."

Curly was warming to his subject once more. For the sake of the immediate peace and tranquility of all concerned, it was fortunate that his listeners, to a man, were from Montana and pronounced cow as to Curly's liking. He was among friends and he proceeded with his enlightening harangue.

"With all due respect to Texas and Texans," he continued, "and giving them all credit due as to their ability as kaouw punchers—I have seen a few Longhorn Texas waddies who did have an idea or two about cattle—but by Cripes when they came up into God's country they dropped their nasal twang and called a cow as it should be called, C-O-W. Any of them, who, after becoming civilized, insisted on calling a cow a kaouw, I have found, were mostly connivin' phonies."

"How about Arkansas and Oklahoma?" some brave soul broke in.

Curly snorted disgustedly. "Not a real cowman in either state," he replied. "Sharecroppers and cotton pickers—Steinbeck will tell you about those birds in his book *Grapes of Wrath.*"

"Where do you suppose those radio and moving picture cowboys come from?" a wee voice ventured from a corner seat.

"Your guess about those lace pants babies is as good as mine, fellow," Curly answered. "I'm a cowman and was raised among cowmen—and that means C-O-W men. Go ask some soda squirt in a drug store, he might have an idea." Curly arose from his seat as a sign that his oration was ended.

Halfway through the door, he paused, as someone turned on the radio.

"Zzzz. Crackle! Crack! I'm an old Kaouw Hand from the Rio Grande," a baritone this time.

The door slammed violently.

Source: William A. Burke

TALES ABOUT THE CHUCKWAGON

*O*ne of the most difficult persons, whose long years of experience and residence in Montana makes him an authority on early day range life, is Joe DeMuth of Belt. The difficulty lies in the fact that he does not want any part of his stories to appear in print. The circumstances in which the following story was gained was mighty far from the range. The story came out of discussing with a group of local residents the present World War. One of them knowing that the writer was an ex-service man asked him if he were a cook in the army. Before I had a chance to reply Joe DeMuth cut into the conversation with a remark:

"Hell, him know how to cook?! I could take one old-time chuckwagon cook and he could feed a regiment where it now takes ten of these tin can grease burners to ruin a pot of coffee." He continued on without anyone interrupting him: "How would you make biscuits without a stove an' oven? You fellows today would starve to death if they quit makin' can openers."

Knowing that the best way to draw him further was to defend the modern cook and at the same time putting him on the defense, I assumed an injured air and indignantly replied, "What the Hell did your chuckwagon boys' have, ham trees and champaign geysers? Just what would your manure smelling biscuit shooters do if the Gerries [Germans] started peppering your slumguilion pot with machine guns just before the noon meal; look for a horse?"

The rest of the group withdrew from the discussion leaving DeMuth and I to carry on. DeMuth deeply engrossed in the righteousness of his cause cried out, "The old-time chuckwagon cook would have better sense than to let himself get caught by the Dutchmans."

After much haranguing on my part, and two bottles of beer and ten minutes later, the old gentleman was pretty well worked up. In reply to the remark: "There is not one outstanding accomplishment worth noting ever made by a chuckwagon cook."

"What do you mean by saying that?" he cried. "Why I can remember back when. . . ."

"You remember what?" I goaded him.

"Why one time out on a roundup over around Geyser our cooky got caught in a stampede."

"When was this?" I interrupted.

"Back in '86 or '87; what the hell difference does it make anyhow? And a bunch of stampedin' cows can do more damage when they're on a rampage than all the armies in Europe. Anyway the cook had on a batch of biscuits."

"I thought you said that he didn't have any oven." I said.

"He didn't; that's what I've been saying—them fellows knew how to get out a meal without all these newfangled ideas. Do you know what a Dutch oven is? By golly they make the best bread in the world in 'em. Anyway as I was sayin', the cook had on a batch of biscuits when all of a sudden hell on hoofs came his way. They was stampedin', Slim (the cook) knowed that he had about ten jobs to do all at once't; getting his four ornery horses away from the wagon, saving his biscuits. What'd you done?"

Without waiting for a reply he continued:

"They was just no use, them cows had him and the chuck wagon in the middle before he could get the horses untied. One of 'em hit that Dutch oven with its dough raw, but hot, and when that hot dough stickin' to its flanks started to be felt the stampede didn't go any further but it kept on stampede'n—right in one spot. That spot was Slim's chuck lay-out. Slim managed to keep himself and his horses from gettin' hurt until the cattle cleared out, and then he went to work straightenin' up the wreck. And by golly inside of an hour and a half he had everything going with a damn good dinner on. I'd like to see any of these can opener cooks do that."

"That's pretty good all right," I replied, "but I can imagine what a hell of a meal it must have been—but I guess that you fellows couldn't't've have told the difference anyway."

"What do you mean we don't know the difference? Say, we

didn't have fried chicken nor fried trout but we did have beef, potatoes, biscuits and coffee—and by golly what coffee! Man, there never was such coffee as what they had in them days, and it didn't come in tin cans either, no sir, it come green; looked like half beans. Slim'd take a couple o'dippers full of that green coffee and roast it in his Dutch oven and he wouldn't let it get cold before he would start grindin' it; you could smell it for twenty miles, and it sure smelt good."

"And of course you must have had angel food cake or Boston creme pie for dessert," I interrupted in an attempt to keep the conversation from growing cold.

"No, we had honey butter and biscuits; what's better dessert than that?"

"That ought to be pretty good," I replied, "but I didn't know your chuckwagon cook carried his own bee hive with him out on the range." His reply brought everyone to their feet laughing.

"Certainly he had his beehive with him!"

"Come, come, Joe. If you don't watch out you'll be chosen as Montana's prize entry to America's liars contest. At the speed you're going you'll be telling us that you broke polar bears to saddle in the Sahara Desert."

"You don't believe he had a beehive, huh? A man is only makin' a fool of himself tryin' to tell you anything. You already know everything; that's the trouble with you fellows. You're too damned smart. Well, he had beehives, anyway he had one beehive and we had honey—and he didn't carry around a bouquet of roses for them to chew on either. No sir, he didn't have to. They was robber bees and they had some damned good scouts with 'em too."

I looked around and addressing no one in particular, said: "Well, fellows, here we go again." And then turning to DeMuth I said: "Go on Joe, this is good, tell us some more about this galley slave-keeper of the bees. This is really interesting. I am sure that no one would want to miss out on hearing about these Jesse James of the apiaries."

"I don't know anything about apes except from watchin' you, but if you think I'm lying about them bees you're crazy. Slim had a beehive all right and he handled 'em better'n some of the boys handled them cows. I never knowed them to stampede on him and that's more than any cow-hand can say about handlin' cows. Why, Slim would have handles at the top of the hive fastened on like the bail of a syrup bucket, only where they fastened onto the hive he would have springs. When he traveled he would hang his hive up on the lantern hook and then he would drive easy like so that they wouldn't get mad or scared. When he set up camp he would put the hive under the chuckwagon. The bees wouldn't do much for the first day but it wouldn't be long until they scattered out and went to work for Slim."

"Yes, yes, go on, Joe."

"That's all, he had bees and we had honey."

"Now, Joe, you started this argument. First you tell us what a great cook this ' Slim' was; before you convince anyone you drift off into a cattle stampede, which turns into a hive of thieving bees, and just when we would like to hear about these bandits you say: ' That's all.' The point that I'm trying to get at is this: Did Slim train them to be honey rustlers or did they learn it from the two-legged company they had to keep?"

"Don't you know that bees are like humans?" he replied. "You won't work for a living if somebody leaves a tub full of money out in his yard, will you? Hell no, and neither will anybody else. And when the money is all gone in the tub you'll look around for another tub instead of goin' to work. Well, bees is the same way. They'll pass up a clover to look for another tub; they're just like humans that-a-way. A funny thing happened once. There was a barber over 'round Stanford that raided a wild bee's nest and got about a hundred pounds of wild honey. He brung it to town in a box and set it out on a lumber pile figurin' that would be a nice cool place until morning. The chuckwagon was only about a mile from town, as we wasn't goin' out on the roundup for about a week. A scout had found the barber's honey cache and come back and led Slim's stingin' *Vinegarones* to it. Slim knowed they was out on the prowl, so he hot-foots it to town. On the way he could look over his head and he would see droves of them going and comin'; they was sure busy. When he got to town everybody was cussin' and swearin'; the bees would get lost in houses and they would smatter up all the windows. It wasn't long until the barber comes runnin' up and tellin' him to do something about it. Slim tells him they can't do anything about it until after dark as the bees won't let nobody get that honey in the daytime. Of course he knows that them bees are workin' for him so what does he care. Well, when night come he goes over and tells the barber that it is safe for him to take his honey inside. When the barber takes hold of that box he braces himself for the strain of it weighed about a hundred pounds the night before. When he picks it up it was like pickin' up a sack full of goose feathers. He was sure surprised. Slim busts out laughin' at him. Them bees didn't leave enough honey to butter a biscuit."

"Go on, Joe, I'm listening."

"Go on yourself, what are you tryin' to tell me to go on for?"

"Ain't you going to tell any more about them bees?" He looked at me very disgustedly and started walking away saying: "I'm not wastin' any more time talkin' to a fool."

As I prepared to leave I said: "So-long, Baron Munchausen."

I overheard him say to the others, "What does he mean by that?"

My parting reply, "Why Baron Munchausen was a chuckwagon cook over on your ancestors' range about three hundred years ago."

Source: Wayndle R. Johnson recorded the above interaction he had with Joe DeMuth, a resident of Montana for sixty years.

AN INCIDENT ON THE RANGE

It was on the roundup on Half Breed Creek in 1903. Jim Bowman, Sam Young, and Tom Shipp were out after a beef for butchering. Jim Bowman threw his rope over a two-year-old heifer. In some inexplicable way in throwing the rope Jim Bowman got the rope tied around the wrist of the hand with which he threw the rope. There was eight feet of rope between his hand and the rope tied to the saddle horn. Bowman seeing his plight suddenly spurred up his horse to keep up with the calf he had roped and keep the rope from pulling tight on his hand. In the meanwhile he got the rope loose from the saddle horn. At a time like this a fast horse was essential to a cowboy.

Tom Shipp noticed Bowman spurring up his horse and maneuvering his arms around in a peculiar fashion. He realized that something had happened to Bowman. Tom Shipp and Sam Young rode quickly to Bowman's assistance. Sam Young roped the heifer but his rope broke. Just as Shipp reached Bowman, Bowman succeeded in getting the rope off of his wrist. Shipp then roped the heifer and threw the heifer just at the door of the cook tent. Bob Carson the roundup cook came out and hit the heifer in the head with an ax. Shipp remarked, "Next time I'll deliver the critter on the stove."

Source: *Tom Shipp of Roundup, Montana*
Collector: *Evelyn M. Rhoden*

THE LITTLE WHITE BULL

I am going to tell you a story about a little white bull, which was owned by T. C. Power of the old Horseshoe Bar ranch on Spring Creek. Maybe the story won't be of any use to you in your work but you said you wanted any kind of a story that had to do with livestock, so I will tell it to you.

Well, the time of this story dates back to about 1885, at which time I was just a young man and very much interested in cattle, though I didn't own any of my own. I was working as a cowboy for Henry Brooks, who was managing the Horseshoe Bar at that time. I was out riding the range, searching for stray cattle during the roundup season of 1885, when I ran across the subject of this story. I was several miles down the creek from the ranch house and had just turned a bend in the creek when I happened to come upon a lone cow, belonging to the Horseshoe Bar outfit. Riding up closer to the cow, I saw that there was a baby calf lying down by her side and the calf was almost as white as snow. Well, that was the first pure white calf I have ever seen. I have seen several almost white calves but they had a little black or brown on them someplace. This calf was white all over and his eyes were red. Even his nose was whitish colored and his hooves were white.

I was riding up to the spot where the calf and cow was, but the cow wanted to protect her baby and I had to rope and tie her down before I could get near the calf. When I did get close, my first thought was that the calf was dead because during the time I spent roping and tieing the mother up, the calf never even raised his head. I walked up to where he was laying and found him to be pretty sick. I don't think he was more than several hours old because his hide was still wet in spots. I guess he hadn't gotten enough to eat either and upon closer examination, I found out the reason why. One of his legs had buckled on him somehow while he was sucking and he had fallen down with the leg under him and wasn't able to get up. I don't know how long the poor little devil had laid there but it must have been for quite a spell because he let out a little squall when I gently straightened the leg out. Then I picked up the little calf and tied him across my saddle skirt. Then untying the mother, I made a leap for my saddle and was away before the cow got to her feet. I rode slowly so the cow could keep up close to me and headed for the ranch house.

After I got to the ranch, I had to figure out some way to get the cow in the corral and keep her there until the calf was strong enough to get around. Well, with the calf still across my saddle, I rode into the largest corral and the cow followed me. After I got to the far side, I turned my horse and sped out, swinging the pole gate on my way out, which fastened by a pole which dropped down over the top pole of the corral. Then jumping off the horse, I fastened the gate securely with a big log chain, hanging around the gate post. I got the calf off the horse and took it into the bunkhouse and laid him on a blanket and went and got some warm milk and fed him. He sure was hungry. I kept rubbing his leg and bending it and seen it was all right and the calf could stand up. After three days, the calf was strong enough to be turned out and I let him go with his mother, after first putting the brand on him. Well, as soon as they were turned out, they took off for someplace and that was the last we saw of the calf for about six months.

Then one day, one of the other men came in and reported seeing a pure white bull running with about twenty head of Horseshoe Bar cattle. He told us there was a stray bull but when the cattle were rounded up, they found out that the white bull was branded with our brand. Finally I told them about the time I found the calf and brought him back to health and branded him. At six months, the bull weighed about 1,100 pounds and was well proportioned. It was then that Mr. Brooks decided to use the white bull for other purposes other than for breeding because the bull was just a range bull and not too good a breeder anyway.

The bull was thrown and cut and from then on, he was trained as a bucking bull and he got to be such a tough character, that there was not a single cowboy on the whole ranch who could ride the white bull to a standstill. It was then that Mr. Brooks got the bright idea that netted the Horseshoe Bar ranch almost $1,500. He began to spread the word around to the various ranches that there would be a $25 reward to the person who could ride the little white bull to a standstill but that there would be a $5.00 entry fee to each person who tried his luck.

Well, I guess every cowboy in the neighboring country tried to ride the bull but failed. The word finally got to other parts of the country, and cowboys from all over the state came to the ranch to try and ride the white bull. But he was so strong and full of life and tricks that none of them ever stayed more than ten or fifteen seconds at the most. Well, the word kept spreading around about the white bull that nobody could ride, and cowboys came from Washington, Oregon, Idaho, Wyoming and even from Utah, and still none of them won the prize money. After a short time, Mr. Brooks raised the prize money but left the entry fee the same. Well, I never met so many strangers in my whole life as I met during just one year at the Horseshoe Bar ranch.

Finally, one day in the early fall of 1886, when the bull was a little over a year old, a tall, skinny young feller came to the ranch from up in Canada and said he would like to try his luck at riding the little white bull. Several of the best men in the country were at the ranch at the time, and when this feller made his intentions clear, they sort of snickered to themselves and felt sorry for him. He looked like the wind could blow him away but he was sincere and paid his $5.00 fee to ride. He never minded any of the kidding he got from the men but joked right back with them and before long had won them over with his sportsmanship. The next day was a Sunday and there was a large crowd gathered to watch the cowboy ride the bull. He got on in the corral chute, and when the gate was throwed open, the bull did everything in his power to loosen the rider but he stuck until the bull was so tired he could hardly move. The cowboy threw his long legs over the bull and slid to the ground with a big grin on his dust-covered face. Sweat was running down his cheeks and forehead but he had done what none of the other could do, and thereby he had won the prize money of $50 and the admiration of every cowboy in the country. He was offered a job on the ranch as a top hand but declined, saying he had a small ranch of his own up in Canada and had just come to Montana for one reason and that was to ride the little white bull he had heard so much about. He had ridden him and was satisfied and then all he wanted was to go back to his ranch. Well, after he had ridden the bull to quits, Mr. Brooks saying he never had any more use for him, gave him the white bull to take to his ranch. The cowboy thanked him and told us all so long and left, driving the bull ahead of him.

Mr. Brooks later figured up and told us he had made $1,450 by charging cowboys a $5 to try and ride the bull. For a common range bull, $1,450 is a lot of money.

Source: *Lem Slater*
Collector: *William Buchanan, Jr.*

THE WRONG TRICK TO PLAY

I'll tell you about a trick which our camp cook tried to play on a bunch of us riders in the early days. The time of this incident was back in 1887, just after the coldest damn winter anybody ever heard about. All the cattlemen were on the rampage because they lost so much stock that winter and they took out all their spite on the riders. This made the riders mad because they knew it wasn't their fault that it got so dadburned cold that all the stock died off; and them that didn't wasn't fit for nothing. Us fellers wasn't in any mood for joking, but it seems that our cook, a feller who we all called Uncle Grayson because he was older than most of us and seemed to like the nickname, was always in a good mood and always liked to put something over on us riders.

Well, come nightfall, here come the whole caboodle of us in to chuck, and when we got our horses unsaddled and fed and watered, we was pretty dogged out. We had put in a hard day. Since before the sun come up that morning until away after it went down, we was going hell for leather, looking for strays and trying to save other critters from dying off. Well, here we comes in to camp, ready for some good grub, which our cook, one of the best, always put out for us. Well, we got our horses put away and went for the old chuckwagon, but we didn't find any cook or nothing to eat. Then we was sore. We were tired and hungry and what a-cussing that cook got from the whole bunch of us. I guess it was about an hour later, when we hears the cook yell, "Come and git it."

Well, he sounded like he was far away and we couldn't tell just what direction the sound come from so we hollered right back and asked where he was but not another sound did he make. We looked all around for him but couldn't find hide nor hair of Uncle Grayson. We was mad enough to eat grass and almost that hungry. Here was the wagon and all the equipment, right where it should be but no fire or no cook and worse still, no grub. Well, we ranted and snorted and cussed Grayson but I guess it didn't do no good and all the while we figured Grayson was hiding some place, snickering to himself about all the fun he was having at our expense. Well, what we didn't think about doing to him when we found him wasn't worth thinking about. We was going to hog-tie him and each one of us was going to smack him across the rump with barrel staves until his rump was so blistered that he wouldn't be able to sit down for a month, and we was just mad enough to do it.

Well, pretty soon, one of the boys found Grayson. Uncle Grayson was quite a feller. He was one of these fellers who can talk and make it sound like it was coming from someplace else. And that is how he fooled us. Why, he wasn't fifty feet away from the camp wagon and it sounded like he was miles away. Well, the feller who caught Grayson threw his rope around him and snubbed him, and the rest of us came a running. The old boy was so scared that he just sat and shook like a newborn calf on a cold morning. Well, we lived up to our word. We spanked him but not so hard as we was a-going to, and he promised he wouldn't ever try to trick us again, so we let him go providing he cooked us the best grub we had had for a long spell. Well, one of the boys built a fire and another peeled spuds. Pretty soon old Grayson had a good meal cooking and it sure tasted good when it was done. The next morning we had bacon and flapjacks and coffee and old Uncle Grayson told us that the only reason he tried to fool us was because it was April 1 and that was All Fool's Day and that we sure was a poor bunch of fools. Well, we forgave the old feller but told him not to ever let it happen again and he said he wouldn't, but all the time he had a big grin all over his fat face just like he was already thinking up something to pull on us.

Well, all went along good as could be and Grayson never once tried to fool us until about two months later when none of us was thinking about anything. We was all in a pretty good mood, even the bosses of our outfits, when one evening after the work was all done, we had put our horses up for the night and was hungry and waiting for the cook to holler, "Come and get it." We was gong to have a beef mulligan for supper, and not having had any stew for quite a spell, it sounded right good. Old Grayson was one man who knew how to make a good mulligan. Well, about fifteen minutes later, Uncle Grayson yelled, "O.K. boys, come and git it while it's hot." And let me tell you, we sure made a bee line for the cook wagon, and man, did it ever smell good. It was made with tender juicy steak, cut from a freshly butchered yearling steer, that morning. It had tomatoes, potatoes, and other vegetables in it and it was good and hot. It also had something else in it. Grayson didn't tell us what it was, but we found out later and didn't git over it for several days. And when we did git over it we could have beat hell out of the old man if we could have found him, but he had pulled stakes for parts unknown, during the night.

Do you know what it was that old Uncle Grayson put in that good mulligan? Sliced soap. Yes, about a whole cake of it. He had that mulligan flavored so good that you couldn't smell or even taste the soap but not long after, you sure knew it was there. All that night and the next day, us fellers was on the jump. There was s--- scattered all over the range. Even our underwear was full of it. Man, we sure was one sick outfit for about a week after that. We was so weak we couldn't hardly walk. We found the note which the old man left pinned to the side of the chuck wagon. This is what he wrote: "I put the soap in the mulligan to git even with a bunch of coyotes who couldn't take a April Fool's joke and almost beat a poor old man to death on account of it. Well, I bet this will fix you. When you find this note, I will be headed for other ranges. I sure will miss you boys."

Well, we was hopping mad until we found that note. But after we read it, I guess all of us felt sort of bad. Well, right then and there, we forgave the old man and asked all over the range, if somebody knew where he was to tell him that he was the best cook in the country, even if he did pull a dirty trick like that and that we would forgive him if he would come back. Well, about two weeks later, he showed up and we sure was a happy bunch of men and gave him a present of a watch. It sure was good to have a good cook back after trying to digest grub which was cooked, in turns, by each rider in the outfit.

Source: William Buchanan, Jr.

A High Price to Pay for a Hard Job

*Y*oung *feller, I'm going to tell you about a young man who had to
pay a mighty big price for a job as a range rider on the spread where
I was working.* You may think that there are real cowboys today, but
let me tell you that there are no riders like there was in the old days.
No sir, lots of these young fellers who claim to be cowboys today
couldn't have gotten a job as a cowboy in those days, when a man
had to be more than a man to even hold down some of the ornery
critters which was running loose on the range. Now, I ain't saying
that these boys today can't ride horses, because they can and they
can ride good, but the horses nowadays ain't as wild and mean as
they was then. No siree, the horses in those days were wild as deer
and just about as fast and smart. They were as thick as flies and
belonged to nobody but the man who caught them and broke them.
But to get back to me story. Now, this ain't no cock and bull story.
It's the honest to God's truth and any of the old timers who were
around at that time will tell you the same story if you ask them.

Now, this young feller's name was Bob Starkel, and he was just
a punk kid, leastwize that is what us older men thought of him
when we first seen him. It was along about the middle of June 1885,
I reckon, when we was all out in the corral, catching our horses for
the day's work. We was just gitting a good start on the summer
roundup and I guess there was about fifty of us men in the outfit.
Well, there was old Dad Pickins. He was cooking for the outfit. Let's
see, there was Jim Newton and Johnny Corbly and Joe Brown and
a whole lot of other cowboys. I can't recollect their names right now
and I guess I have forgotten lots of their names, but they were all
good men and as tough as they come. We was all working for the
Horseshoe Bar outfit and old Johnny Brooks was managing it. He
was a real man and knew how to pick the men he wanted on his
payroll, and when he told a man he could have a job, he meant it
and the same goes for when he told a man he was fired and to go

git his wages. If old Brooks liked a man, he was a real friend, but if he didn't like a man, that man had a bad enemy. As far as I know, Brooks never had an enemy in his life because he was always a cheerful and kind-hearted man and nobody had any room to dislike him.

Well, as I said, we was all out in the corral, bright and early that June morning and was just about to eat breakfast when this kid walks up and says, "Morning, gents." Well, we all said good morning and asked him a couple of questions and he told us the answers. Now, Johnny Corbly thought the kid was pretty young and Corbly was not too old himself. He was about twenty-five, I reckon and he says to the kid, "Ain't you kinda scared to be around all these horses and as scared to be away from your momma?"

The kid eyed Corbly for a minute and said in a low voice, "No, I ain't scared to be around these horses and I ain't afraid of anyone who rides on top of them either." Well sir, Corbly didn't know what to say to that so he starts to peel his jacket off and the kid does likewise. Well, the next few minutes, dust is flying and when it clears away, Corbly is laying out cold as a doornail on the ground and young Bob is standing over him. Well, we manage to git the kid in a friendly mood again and after Johnny comes to, he apologized to the kid and from then on, they was as good a buddies as you'd ever want to see.

We asked the kid how old he was and he told us he was twenty-two and asked us where the boss was because he needed a job. We told him the boss would be around in a few minutes and that he better have a bit to eat before he asked the boss for a job because riding herd on cattle all day on an empty stomach ain't no fun. None of us expected old Brooks to give the kid a job because he looked just like a punk kid. He was about five foot seven inches tall and was of slim build, but he was as strong as hell and not afraid of anything. Well, about ten minutes later, old Brooks comes down to the corral and looks all of us over and finally notices the kid standing with his back to the chuck wagon, rolling a cigarette as any man would, and trying to look older than he was and still be himself. He wasn't having much luck with his cigarette because he didn't smoke and had never tried to roll a cigarette before. That's what he told us after he had been with the outfit for a few weeks. Well, Brooks walked over to where the kid was standing and looked him over. It kinda got on the kid's nerves or something because he looked Brooks right in the eye and asked him what he was looking at. A question like that, coming from a young kid, kinda got Brook's dander up for a minute but he soon cooled off or at least we thought he had when he asked the kid what he was doing here and what he wanted.

The kid said, "Mr. Brooks, my name is Bob Starkel and I'm looking for a job. I got a sick mother and I got to look after her."

Brooks looked at Bob again and said, "You look kinda small to be asking for a job. Can you ride?"

"Sure, I can ride."

"Well," said Brooks, "we'll see if you can ride. Johnny, toss your rope around Blackie's neck. Ed, you and Jim, saddle the horse. Bob here is going to ride him."

We thought Brooks was kidding us for a minute and none of us moved. "Well, what are you waiting for?" asked Brooks, "I said to saddle Blackie so Bob here can show us how he can ride."

Now we all knew that Blackie was a killer and there had never been a man yet that could git on him and stay there for more than a second. We all tried to talk Brooks out of it and to give the kid another horse but he had his mind set on Blackie, so there wasn't nothing we could do about it but saddle the horse. Johnny threw his rope over the black's head and Jim and me threw a blindfold over his eyes to keep him from seeing the saddle. Several of the boys got around Bob and tried to talk him out of riding the horse, but he was determined to ride him if it killed him. We all thought that that was just what would happen if he did git on the horse and told him so, but it didn't do no good because he needed a job and if he had to ride a horse to git the job, ride that horse he would. Well, Brooks came over then and asked the kid if he still wanted a job and the kid said yes.

Well, Johnny snubbed Blackie to a corral post while the kid got in the saddle and told Bob not to try to ride because there had been more than one man tried it and come out loser and suffered from broken backs, arms and legs but Bob just grinned at Johnny and said, "Pull the blinders."

As soon as the blind came off, Bob dug his spurs deep into Blackie's flanks and began fanning him with his hat and yelling. Blackie stood still for about a second and then let loose. He changed ends so fast that nobody saw him turn. He sunfished and stiff-legged high into the air and before he came down again, he had switched ends and lit stiff-legged. The jolt brought big beads of sweat on Bob's face but he was still in the saddle. Blackie jumped almost before his feet would touch the ground and kept wondering why that thing on his back did not fall off. He had never had anything on his back for more than a second and he showed plainly, he didn't like it. He had tried everything to git the man off of his back but it hadn't worked. He had one more trick and that was to go over backwards and roll on his rider. By this time, Brooks was as scared as any of us and kept yelling for the kid to git off and that the job was his but the kid either didn't hear him or was riding from just plain nerve. Any other man would have been knocked senseless from all those jolts, but not the kid. No sir, he was still in the saddle and still flanking the horse and fanning him with his hat although his face was as red as blood and the cords on his neck stood out like they was about to break.

Well, Blackie reared up on his hind legs and went over backwards. We all yelled for the kid to git off, and when he didn't, we expected him to be crushed by the weight of the horse. Brooks was almost crying because he knew he was the cause of all of it and would never forgive himself if anything happened to the kid. Well, most of us turned our heads when Blackie went over and was afraid to look up but we sure got the surprise of our lives when we did because there was the kid, still in the saddle and Blackie was trotting around the corral. The horse was as thoroughly beaten as was Johnny Corbly, a few moments before. A horse knows when he is licked and when he has found his master and Blackie knew he had found his. Blackie was as gentle as a baby lamb from then on, but there was nobody on that roundup who could ride the horse, even then. He was a one man horse and to show how much he admired the man who had broken him, Blackie followed Bob around just like a dog. He was as faithful to his master as a horse can be and Bob was proud of being the only man who had ever been able to ride the horse.

Well, Brooks became very fond of the kid after that and the kid liked Brooks. He got his job and was one of the best riders and cowboys who ever rode a horse. Not only did Brooks give the kid a job but to show how much he thought of young Bob, he gave him Blackie as a present and told him that as long as he wanted work, he could have a job on the spread. Bob soon became one of the bunch and was liked and admired by every man in the outfit. He saved his money and took care of his sick mother and sent her to a hospital where she was well taken care of.

The last time I saw Bob was in 1915. He had stopped riding and was in the farming business out on Warm Springs Creek. We got together and talked about the early days and the good old times we used to have when we worked as saddle partners in the early days on the Horseshoe Bar. I believe that Bob is dead now because I never hear of him from anyone, but he was one of the best and squarest men I ever knew.

Source: Ed Silverthorne was a friend of Bob Starkel and a past employee of the Horse-shoe Bar.

Collector: William Buchanan, Jr. Mr. Buchanan notes that the above story was verified by Patrick McEnerney and Johnny Gilkerson, both friends of Bob Starkel. Bob
Brooks, a son of old John Brooks, also verified the story for Mr. Buchanan.

FOUR HUNDRED DOLLARS FOR A FIFTY-DOLLAR HORSE

*M*aybe this isn't just the kind of a story you are looking for, but it
deals with the early days in Fergus County and with livestock.
This story is about a three-year-old horse that I raised from a baby
colt. There was nothing out of the ordinary about this horse. He
was just a common colt born of a range mare, but he was a beauty.
His body was long and slender and his legs were long and small.
Well sir, I halter broke the horse before he was five months old and
taught him to wear a saddle and bridle. I never rode the horse until he was almost a year old and when I got on him he never even
let out one jump. I never scolded him or whipped him. He never
bucked or balked and was not shy of anything.

I rode the horse for two years and was riding him in Lewistown
one day in 1895. Everyone who saw the horse wondered where in
the world I ever got hold of such a beautiful horse. His hide was
sleek and his color a chestnut brown. His forelegs were white and
he had a white star on his forehead. He looked and carried himself
just like a thoroughbred racehorse. Well, old Nate McCauley, a
stockman from the Forest Grove section, happened to see me riding
past the Post Office and yelled at me to pull up and talk a spell. I
didn't have anything important to do at the moment, so I got off
the horse and walked over to the porch of the Post Office and sat
down and we began talking. I kept noticing that McCauley kept
his eyes on the horse and he, being a lover of horses, asked me what

I wanted for him. I told him the horse wasn't for sale but I needed a couple of good work horses and if he would consider a trade, of my own picking, he could have the horse. Well, he scratched his head for a few minutes and got up and walked out to where the horse was and began to give him the once over. He looked at his legs and felt of them, he looked at his eyes, nose and mouth, his shoulders and finally his teeth. Finding everything to be in good shape, McCauley came back to the porch and said I had made a deal and for me to come to his place the next day and select any two of his horses I wanted for my horse and a bargain would be made. He would have all of his horses rounded up and I could do my own choosing. That sounded fair enough to me and I felt sort of elated to think that I had pulled a fast one on a man who was supposed to be an expert on horseflesh. I knew that my horse's looks was what sold McCauley and not the breed. Why, that horse of mine wasn't worth over fifty dollars but I wasn't gong to tell McCauley that.

Well, the next day, I went over to McCauley's ranch and began looking over his horses. After a few hours of looking and feeling them out, I finally picked out two mares to my suiting. They were big-boned and weighed about 1,100 pounds. They were just what I was looking for.

Well, we drew up papers on the deal and shook hands in friendship. He asked me if my horse could run and I told him I didn't know. He said the horse looked like a runner and I knew right then that McCauley had not been so dumb. I never ever thought of making a racehorse out of my horse. McCauley said he would soon see if the horse could run or not, and if he could, he would make a lot of money on him at the county fairs. Well, three months later, McCauley met me on the street in Lewistown and told me that he had just won $75 in a race. He said he had a fine horse and was going to make a lot more money before the year was out. I told him that was fine and I meant it too. Well, about two weeks later, I met a buyer from North Dakota who was looking for good horseflesh and I told him about my team of horses. He said he would come out to look them over and if he bought them he would pay me highest prices for them.

The next day he came out to my place, and after looking them over offered me $400 cash for the two. Well, I naturally jumped at the chance to sell the horses and the deal was completed as soon as possible in order that the buyer would not change his mind about buying them. Well, the papers were made out and I had $400 in my hand. The next day I went into Lewistown and there I met McCauley. He was as mad as a hornet and asked me if I wanted to trade horses back. I told him no and asked him what was the matter. He said that since the horse won that $75 awhile back, he had not been able to ever get the horse to run again. He had tried everything he knew to make the horse run but it was just no go. The horse refused to run. He even had hired a jockey to ride the horse but that wasn't any good either so now he wanted to get rid of him. Well, I couldn't help but grin and when he saw me grinning he asked me what was so funny. I told him I couldn't trade back even if I wanted to, because I had just made a deal with a buyer from North Dakota for the horses and had been paid $400 in cash for them. He sure blew up then. He raved and snorted all over Lewistown and the next time I saw him, which was a few hours later, he was as drunk as hell and about as ornery. He was cussing that horse for all he was worth and offered to sell him to the first man who wanted him. Well, I walked up to McCauley and offered him $100 for the horse and he jumped at the chance to get rid of him. Well, the deal was made right there and witnessed by several men who were standing around. I paid McCauley the $100 and still had $300 left and my original saddle horse. So I guess I was not so dumb as I thought I was.

Several days later, I met McCauley again and he was in gay spirits to know that I had my horse back and he had $100 even if he had been bested in our first deal. After that, we were very good friends and never had any trouble, but we never did any more trading of horses thereafter.

Source: William "Bill" Wendt of Judith Place, Lewistown, Montana
Collector: William Buchanan, Jr.

"HORSE-CHOKE" DAY

*T*his is a story that seems more like a tall tale then the truth, but is sworn to, as being the truth by several persons who were living at the time it happened.

Out in the country near the town of Judith Gap, a man by the name of John Day was running a horse ranch. He was a breeder of fine-blooded horses and purchased purebred stallions to cross with his mares. It seems there were many wild horses around the country in those days, which was in 1883, and these wild horses would break into Day's pastures, where he kept his brood mares, and mate with them. Day became suspicious of this when he found that six of his mares were being trailed by six range colts and decided to do something about it.

One summer night, Day brought in thirty-five of his mares and penned them up, then seeking a good hiding place, proceeded to watch for any happenings. He had a very fast saddle horse tied nearby in case he needed one. Then along about 11:30 that night, his saddle horse whinnied and Day was all alert. Very soon, he spotted a few horses and knew that they were not his. On closer scrutiny, he found them to be wild stallions, which made him very mad. He quietly got his saddle horse and started after the wild stallions.

Very shortly, he came alongside one of the stallions and immediately roped the animal and before he had stopped him, he jumped onto his back and with his two arms, choked the stallion to death. Day is the only man known who ever had the strength to choke a wild mustang. Day was a man about six feet, four inches tall and he weighed close to 350 pounds. He was not afraid of man or beast and was never bluffed by anything.

He is reputed to have killed at least twenty wild stallions by choking them with his hands. He was called by those who knew of his feats, "Horse-Choke" Day.

Sources: Tom Gregory, a friend of Day's, and B. F. Gordon, the son of the man who bought Day's ranch

COOKY

*O*ne of the favorite stories told at roundups and other gatherings is of the party of campers who were up in the hills hunting. It had been agreed that the cook was to be chosen by lot and that the first person who found any fault with the cuisine would thereby be elected to serve as the cook in turn. Everything went well for about a week. The cook to whom the lot fell seemed to be entirely satisfactory in all ways whether or not he tried to be. No matter if the spuds were a bit raw or the bacon slightly scorched, everyone seemed to enjoy his cooking with gusto. At last, seeing that he was apt to spend all his camping trip as cooky, the cook became desperate as to ways or means of getting his patrons to find some fault with his culinary ability. So one morning he cooked a big pot of beans for dinner. He made them as appetizing as he knew how and then opening a new box of salt, he dumped the entire box of salt into the bean stew. The campers would either have to eat the beans or find some way to eat elsewhere without kicking against the camp grub. So when dinnertime came each camper found a big bowl of bean stew at his plate. All sat down and dipped their spoons into the savory dish and tasted, and suddenly one man spoke up: "Boy, these beans sure are salty." Then catching the cook's eye hopefully regarding him he added hastily, "but that's just the way I like 'em." And he went on sipping till the last drop was gone!

Source: *Elmer Baird of Roundup, Montana*

STEW MEAT

It was to be one of the big general roundups with outfits from most of Montana east of the Rockies taking part. First to arrive at the location were two cowboys and their duffle wagon from the Marias. These two cowboys proceeded to get the camp into shape and then there was nothing to do but wait for the other outfits to arrive.

The first day they were waiting they spent in exploring the region for many miles around, and they rode into camp that night confident that there would be at least a dozen other outfits to keep them company and start things rolling in the morning. But what was their disappointment to find the camp as quiet and lifeless as when they had left in the morning, and what was most discouraging was a slow drizzling rain set in about sundown. It was a dismal outlook and if they had not come nearly two hundred miles to get there, they would have packed up their wagons and set out for their home outfits on the Marias without waiting any longer.

The next day the rain poured and drizzled by turns and the cowboys could do nothing to amuse themselves, till at last they noticed the many prairie dogs near the camp. Thereafter they amused themselves shooting prairie dogs till by the time it stopped raining they had quite a number of dead prairie dogs to their credit. Then one of them looked at the other with a wink and said, "I wonder if prairie dogs wouldn't be good to eat if they were stewed?"

The other cowboy winked back and drawled, "Now I shouldn't wonder but what they might be."

Without further discussion they set to work and skinned a number of the dead animals and cut them up into a kettle, and in an hour or two there came the unmistakable odor of savory stew from the camp stove. At this time there also came the shouts of riders and rattle of duffle wagons as the long waited roundup crew came into camp, most of them hungry from long hours on the trail. The two first arrivals bustled around setting out cups and plates and soup bowls into which they poured generous helpings of stew for the hungry arrivals.

The newcomers accepted the stew with fervent thanks. They had been riding through the rain and were chilled and tired. "How's for some more of the soup, fellows? Boy, that stuff sure hits the spot. Give me a third helping will you fellows?"

The two cowboys winked at each other and grinned as one of them said in a low voice, "Prairie dogs sort of take the prize as soup meat. But if we value our health we'd better keep still about this for a while, seeing as how they know we had plenty of beef in our wagon to make a stew of."

So it was several days later that they told the men what kind of stew they had eaten, and the men would not believe even then till they had shown the skins of the prairie dogs!

Source: Elmer Baird of Roundup, Montana

OUTBIKING A BOVINE

It was in the days following the World War and Mrs. Angle's husband was a disabled veteran, thus making it necessary for her to earn the bread and butter for their small family, so she applied for and received a job as census-taker. Naturally her work required her to visit many ranches long distances apart, and for this purpose she bought a bicycle to travel on. Having herself just recovered from a siege of illness she had sought the census job on the advice of her doctor who thought the outdoor exercise would be beneficial to her health. So one day after she had visited the home of a rancher far out on the prairie and was winsomely peddling her way down the road, which at this point was bordered by a barbed wire fence, suddenly her poise was rudely disturbed by the loud bellow of a bovine critter behind her. Turning she saw a very large bull galloping along behind her on the other side of the fence. She also realized that at their present rate of progress the critter would pass her, or worse still, take time to jump over the fence, and therewith she gave up further imaginings and applied herself to the task of putting more distance between herself and the creature. The wheels of the bike fairly hummed as she shifted into "high" and applied the pressure to the pedals and the dust made a long low streak down the road. She looked back hoping that the bull had been left far behind, but that quadruped had also shifted into "high" and was closer than before. Not only was he closer but he was giving vent to bellows suggestive of bovine rage and tossing horns. She peddled even faster, if that were possible, but the bull only ran that much faster, till at last out of sheer exhaustion she slowed down. Let him do his worst! But the bull had given up just in time!

Source: *Alma Angle*
Collector: *Elmer Baird of Roundup, Montana*

CHRONIC GROUCH

A *certain crabby old rancher had the name of being a chronic knocker among the ranchers of the Roundup region.* Finally as a sort of joke among themselves, the cowboys and ranchers posted a reward for the first man to hear the crabby knocker say a good word about anybody. The amount of the reward was fifty dollars. Time went on and most everybody forgot about the reward. A year or two passed with nobody ever claiming the money.

In the neighborhood of Gage lived a young man who had been sent to Billings to jail for stealing. The young man escaped with a youthful companion and returned to his home neighborhood where he rounded up a band of horses and hit for the hills. The owner of the horses however happened across the band and hurried to town where he called out a deputy sheriff, collected a posse, and cornered the fugitives on top of a big rock. In the three-day siege that took place the young rustler was shot and his youthful companion captured. As it turned out the twelve-year-old youth that was captured had ran away from home in Ohio to seek his brother "out West" and one of the men in the posse was the brother he was seeking. In the excitement that followed this discovery several of the men started talking about the young man who had been shot to death, and mention was made of some of his better qualities such as his being afraid of nobody and being kind-hearted, etc. After the talk had died down a bit one of the listeners rose to his feet and looked around at the gathering and then down at the chronic grouch.

"I here and now claims I am qualified to receive the fifty-dollar reward for hearing our neighbor speak a good word for anybody. I just heard him say as how Lon (the dead rustler) wasn't such a bad fellow as he might-a been. And therefore I am the first person to hear him say a good word for anybody."

Source: Elmer Baird of Roundup, Montana

Wagonwheel John's First Prisoner

ohn Zimmerman (Wagonwheel John), first sheriff-elect of Teton County, stepped off the train and looked around for some mode of conveyance to take him out to the ranch where the man he was after for stealing a horse was working. Sheriff Zimmerman was disappointed at the size of Malta and its lack of equine habitants. He went to the section foreman's house to see if he could locate a horse.

Why yes, he had a horse to rent, the section foreman answered, but the price would be ten dollars as this was a very extraordinary horse.

Well this was an emergency and so with only a few words of protest Wagonwheel John paid the ten dollars after which the foreman led him to the barn and brought out the horse. One look at the horse convinced Sheriff Zimmerman that it was indeed an extraordinary horse. It resembled a cross between an Ozark mule and a Texas longhorn as it shuffled dejectedly out of the barn and stood with its head down as though ashamed of itself. Sheriff John swung into the patched up saddle and found that a number of tacks had been driven into the seat at the points of closest contact, and at the same time the animal came to life and decided to show the world that it was not to be trifled with no matter if it were a bit off color as to pedigree. Sheriff John did not claim to be any rider and therefore did not disdain to grab the saddle horn with a fervent grip, and the last the section foreman saw of them, they were galloping merrily away toward the wide open spaces, stopping only now and then for a round of bucking during which both man and horse showed their mettle.

A few days later a stranger rode into Malta and in answer to a query he said, "I'm Sheriff John's prisoner. He's back there saddle-sore from riding that cross between a buzz saw and a cyclone that he said you rented to him as a horse. He told me to wait here for him and I reckon I will, cause any man that would ride that critter as far as he has would be useless to try to get away from." And that was how first sheriff-elect Wagonwheel John brought in his first prisoner.

Source: Elmer Baird of Roundup, Montana

Open House

*I*t was the boast of Blaine County pioneer residents that locks and keys were unknown articles during the early settlement era of the district. A free and open range country, it was the ideal territory for hardy men who sought adventure in the open spaces. Cowboys, freighters, and miners made old Chouteau County one of their favorite camping grounds prior to the coming of the homesteader.

Scattered as they were far north of the Milk River Valley, and exposed to the elements on those sweeping, unsheltered prairies, which today are being farmed to sheep, the first ranchers observed a range code of honor that made locks unnecessary. In those days the men of the open range were exposed to great hardships during the severe winter season, and every ranch was "open house" to the rider who sought food and shelter for himself and saddle horse. Every rider of the range knew that this hospitality was an absolute necessity in that country of long distances, and it was the unwritten law that every man's house and food supply was at the disposal of his fellow man at all times. A cowboy, cold and hungry after a hard day's ride, felt no embarrassment in approaching a strange house. If no one happened to be at home, it didn't make a particle of difference, as the visitor was perfectly welcome to stoke up the fire and cook a meal.

One drastic rule did exist, however, in connection with the

"open house" custom of the range, and that was that no visitor could in honor leave dirty dishes behind him after partaking of another rancher's victuals. It was an established and rigidly adhered to custom, and the man who ignored it was liable to find himself in bad standing with the other residents of rangeland.

A legend exists in the Harlem-Turner country that has been handed down from the first settlers who located cattle and sheep ranches in the Woody Island district (thirty-five miles north of Harlem). The following tale has been unfolded so many times by the district pioneers that there must be at least a modicum of truth in it.

In the fall of 1889, a rough and tough character known as Bull Creek Miller came into the sparsely settled country now known as Woody Island. Canada had been his last permanent place of residence and the few Montana men who were living south of the boundary line suspected that he was wanted by the Dominion police. However, few questions were asked strangers in those days, and "Bull Creek" was accepted as a man and given work by American ranchers. He was surly and unsociable, but a good rider and roper, so his unappealing personality did not interfere with his employment. He lived with a cowman named Davis, but was a frequent visitor at all the ranches in the territory, as his duties took him on long rides over the prairies.

After he had been in Montana six months, several ranchers reported the loss of valuable saddle horses. As no trace of the missing animals could be found, these stockmen suspected that a gang of Canadian horse thieves was operating in Montana, riding over at night and getting back into Canadian territory with the stolen animals before daylight. Bull Creek Miller disappeared after one particularly big horse steal had been made, and the ranchers decided that he was implicated. They formed a posse and set out on fresh horses to hunt the rascal down. When near the Canadian line they met another Montana rancher riding south who reported that his top saddle horse, a sorrel gelding, had been stolen the night before.

"Bull Creek Miller was seen near my place yesterday afternoon, and I believe he's the man who made off with the sorrel," stated the rancher whose name was Hodgins. "I reckon I'll ride with you gents across the line, as that's where we'll find him."

The party now numbered seven men, and just as they neared the International boundary they came upon Miller, afoot and limping badly. The scene was near what is now known as Lone Pine Coulee, named for a solitary pine tree that, through some freak of nature, had been able to derive sustenance from the sage-infested soil of that neighborhood. Bull Creek looked sad and crest-fallen and did not offer to speak as the riders rode up on him.

"Hey there, Bull Creek Miller," shouted Hodgins, "my old sorrel piled yuh, did he? That old hoss never did like the smell of horse thieves."

"Yeh, he piled me all right, but you ain't got any kick comin' now. The sorrel pulled south and he'll be home when you get there."

The stern-faced Davis, with whom Miller had lived, spoke in biting terms to the renegade. "We know now that you've been abusing our hospitality, and it would be ruinous to the country to turn you loose and let you join up with your Canadian partner." He turned and faced his fellow-ranchers. "What will we do with him?" he asked.

The Vigilantes were not in force in that part of the country but that little band of cowmen considered themselves a well-constituted court of law. They discussed the matter for a few minutes and decided to leave the decision as to Bull Creek Miller's punishment to Dave Hodgins, the seventh member of the party. That gentleman dismounted and approached Miller, who stood shorn of all the defiance he had formerly shown in the district. "Answer my questions," commanded Hodgins, "and don't forget that your answers will decide your fate. Did you steal my sorrel?"

Well, I took your hoss all right," replied Miller, "but now that he's piled me and gone back to your ranch, you ought to call the matter finished."

"Did you help a gang steal other horses here during the last six months?" inquired Hodgins.

"Yes, I was working with a gang. But hell, Hodgins, there's no great crime in stealing a few cayuses, is there?"

"Well, we might overlook that part, but there's another question I want to ask you. Did you eat at my place yesterday before you made off with the sorrel?"

"Yes, I sure did. Nobody was home so I cooked a meal."

"Can you read?"

"Yes."

"Did you see a sign on the wall of the table?"

"Yes, I noticed a dirty sign hanging there, but I didn't pay much attention to it."

"Well, that's where you made your big mistake. The horse stealin' might be overlooked, but the way you behaved in my cabin settles the matter. Am I to make the final decision on Miller's punishment, gents?" Six heads nodded in assent, and Dave Hodgins, grim and unrelenting arbiter of justice, solemnly pointed to the Lone Pine.

The coyotes on the barren bench-lands surrounding the spot sang Bull Creek's requiem that night.

Tradition has it that the seven horsemen returned south by way of Hodgins' cabin. The six who had originally set out on Miller's trail eagerly looked for the sign on the cabin wall. Begrimed with the smoke of many burned flap-jacks, its crude lettering still was legible, and showed that Hodgins, besides being a stern dispenser of justice and a firm supporter of rangeland etiquette, was no mean hand at formulating a poetic warning to those who sought his hospitality when he was away from home:

If you are hungry, grab a plate,
You have my best of wishes;
But jes' before you pull your freight
Be shore to wash the dishes.

Source: W. H. Campbell of Chinook, Montana

THE WANDERING FORTUNETELLER

The arrival of Professor Tagsdall in Harlem, when the placid life was at an unusually low ebb, created quite a stir among the ladies on the plains. His circulars mailed to all ranch homes in the district appealed to women to meet him in Harlem as he "possessed a message of vital importance for them."

Ranchers were besieged by their wives to drive to town on the day Professor Tagsdall designated for his readings. Buggies, spring wagons and old-style lumber wagons arrived in Harlem early. At 9 o'clock the Professor received his first client in the room he had engaged in the old New England hotel. Six feet in height and extremely slender, with coarse unprepossessing features, Tagsdall resembled an old-time barnstorming "ham" actor. His clothes were threadbare and shoes encasing his large feet were sadly down at the heel. The Professor gave consultations to twenty ranch women that morning, and each of them received the same advice for the fee of five dollars. The Professor's harangue, delivered after an impressive waving of hands was as follows:

"Now my dear lady, it's most fortunate that you came to see

me today. You are about to profit from an extraordinary boom that will place your husband among the rich and respected men of the valley. You must no longer resign yourself to the drudgery of a ranch home. Hire domestics to do your household work, and discard today those shabby old-fashioned clothes that you wear in the name of economy. Do not delay in changing the manner of your living. Procure new hats, dresses, shoes—in fact all wearing apparel that you need. Izzy Koch across the street has a splendid assortment of ladies' wear. Assert your independence today and go home garbed in a complete new wardrobe. Thank you, Madam, and will you tell the next lady to come in?"

At two o'clock that afternoon, Izzy Koch, the little Hebrew merchant, entered the Last Chance Saloon where the ranchers were congregated, with a thick sheaf of charge slips. Each rancher produced his checkbook, paid for his wife's purchases. When they emerged from the saloon the ranchers were confronted with a parade of beauty and finery such as the range country had never seen, displaying hats and dresses of old vintage, but alluring to those women of simple tastes unaware of current boulevard fashions, who promenaded the wooden sidewalks of the town as proud as peacocks. The ranchers, feeling "done in" by Tagsdall but jovial withal to see their wives dressed up for once, escorted the Professor into the Last Chance, and pressed liquor upon him.

The Professor drank copiously and from the bar proclaimed that he was a great benefactor of human kind.

"You gents have got to agree that I pulled off a big stroke of business today," he said. "And the best part of it is that everybody (hic) has benefitted. Your women had become slaves to economy, and I know in your hearts that you want them to splurge once in a while and dress in a way befitting the wives of prosperous ranchers. Little Izzy had a big stock of woman's wear that wouldn't move. He agreed to give me twenty percent if I'd clear it out for him. Well, Izzy hasn't got as much as a ladies' chemise left in stock. I'm well satisfied with the day's work, and as I said before, everybody concerned has benefitted. I must bid you good-day, gents, and thanks for the stimulants. There's another (hic) Izzy waiting for me in Havre."

Professor Tagsdall, uncertain of foot, but whistling merrily as he clutched a man-sized bank roll, staggered out of the Last Chance to board the westbound stage.

Source: Frank Connelly of Harlem, Montana, participated in the episode described above.
Collector: W. H. Campbell of Chinook, Montana

THE THING AT THE FOOT OF THE BED

There is quite a tendency toward jokes of a Paul Bunyan nature given a cowcamp twist. Typical is that of the cowboy who made his bed on the prairie and woke up to find that a rattlesnake had coiled up on his bosom to keep warm during the night. Another is of a cowboy who had went to bed in an old abandoned cabin and woke up sometime during the night to see a weird form leering at him over the foot of his bed. His foot was asleep and so he wasn't quite sure whether it was his own foot or if it was some intruder from the unknown. Anyhow he cautiously drew his trusty six-shooter from under his pillow and took careful aim and said, "Hey, you, if you're what I think you are, why it's gonna be too bad for you. But if you're not what I think you are, why it's gonna be bad for me!"

Source: Elmer Baird of Roundup, Montana

CALDWELL HOMESTEADERS

*A*t the time the land in Caldwell was homesteaded, I ran four bands
of sheep which ranged all over the present thickly settled section.
On the day the Caldwell brothers from Idaho arrived on their fil-
ings, which was where the town now stands, I had a herder with a
flock camped in the center of their claims. The day was hot, and
during the noon hour the herder became sleepy and he laid down
in the grass. He was soon asleep and remained sound in slumber
until along about five in the afternoon. Upon awakening he sat up,
rubbed his eyes, and was at once the most astounded man in the
United States. Gazing in all four directions, he beheld sod houses
upon the roofs of which men labored in feverish haste in laying the
final tiers of sod. The Caldwells had brought a number of young
relatives with them, and with this big crew, they had worked won-
ders while Bill Brant, the herder, was rocked in the arms of
Morpheus. Bill had often heard of herders going suddenly insane.
He knew that the loneliness of his calling, combined with the si-
lence of the prairies, could work havoc on the mental condition of
some men. He had seen sheep herders taken to town drivelling
idiots, and he was now fully convinced that he had joined the ranks
of the "locoed."

Half-reluctantly he made his way to one of the sod structures.
He was greeted with a cheery "halloa" from the men on the roof.
One of the Caldwell brothers told Bill that they had filed on the
land, and intended to produce wheat on it. Bill Brant immediately
transferred his suspicions of insanity from himself to these four
loony brothers who contemplated turning a sheep range into wheat
fields.

Well, the Caldwells lived in their sod houses for several years,
and were successful farmers, one of them winning a state award
for the high quality of his wheat. The same buildings stand today.
They are used as store-houses etc., in rear of where wooden

structures have been put up. These buildings are over twenty years old and are still substantial and weatherproof, and they form excellent monuments to the memory of men who were not thwarted by limited funds in their determination to transform a wild, previously unproductive area into a prosperous farming section. Up to the time of the Caldwell's arrival, all we old-timers would have agreed with Bill Brant that a man was surely insane to try to farm that country.

Source: George Petrie of Turner, Montana, was one of the earliest sheep ranchers of the northern Blaine District.
Collector: W. H. Campbell of Chinook, Montana

FUN WITH TENDERFOOTS

CATTLE BRANDS

Many a dogie# (not "doggie",-dudes please note) has been decorated with one of these famous Montana irons.

CA	Running CA	=Ö=	Two pole pumpkin	ᗯ	Seven VM	✿	Bug
79	Seventy nine	N-N	N bar N	ଅ	Shaving mug	Ữ	Quarter Circle U
D-S	DHS	⊥	Turkey track	40	Forty	Ⓒ	Circle C
⁚⁚	Three Circle	ꓤF	Monogram FUF	LU	LU bar	SH	Monogram SH
⚶	Square and Compass	⌂X	Hat X	⊤	Umbrella	⦋	Bar R
⋊	Long X	⚘	Rocking chair	⇞	Spearhead	0	Flying D
═	Railroad track	▽	Bull head	777	Three sevens	℗	Lazy P swinging
⫤	Lazy H hanging two	ヨ2	Reversed E two bar	⋅⋅	Two dot	Ψ	Antler
⊞	Monogram PLE	VVV	Three V's	⊞	Maltese cross	2A	Two A bar
℧	Horseshoe bar	Ψ	Pitchfork	⚲	Hash knife	⋀	Rafter circle
Ⅳ	N bar	7-7	Seven bar seven	X	Hour glass	⋒	Piece of pie
⅃X	Inverted TX	⊛	Circle diamond	₽	Fish hook	⊖	Mill iron
W	W bar	O	Circle	∪	U lazy J	XIT	
CK		IX		OW		SL	
JO		LO		707		WM	

#A dogie is a little calf who has lost its mammy and whose daddy has run off with another cow.

Montana Highway
Commission roadside
marker near Miles City,
Montana.

Farm Security Administration,

photo by Arthur Rothstein (#46)

CHARLEY RUSSELL AND THE TENDERFOOTS

I worked for a while on a ranch in the Judith Basin country. There's where I met and worked with Charley Russell, the artist. After a roundup, a bucking contest, branding, or most anything that happened on the range, you would see Charley in the bunkhouse that evening with some wrapping paper and a pencil a-drawing what took place. Most everybody remarked when they observed his drawings that they were very true to life.

What I wanted to tell you was what a jobber Charley was. There was a tenderfoot came to the ranch one day, and he was crazy to learn to ride horses. He took to Charley right away. Russell took great care in explaining everything about the West to the novice from the East. The principle worry to the tenderfoot was if he should get bucked off, what could he do to stick to the saddle.

"Well," drawls Charley, "we have a method we always use for you fellas and it works everytime."

"What is it?" eagerly asked the tenderfoot.

"We generally use molasses. Smear some on the saddle seat. You know, it'll hold you in the saddle when the horse wants to throw you out."

"Where can I get some?"

"Oh, from the cook at the chuckwagon. But I think he's about out of it. Better run over and see."

With that the tenderfoot would be off like a flash. I and the rest of the boys were wise to Charley's tricks and knew he'd put something over on the newcomer sooner or later. We'd work right along with him. Of course it was all we could do to keep from laughing right out loud.

The tenderfoot came back with the can of molasses and went through the prescribed course. Naturally, he'd get throwed. Sometimes we would substitute Charley's best saddle for the old one he had on the horse. This was jobbing Charley, and if he caught it in time, he would suddenly order the tenderfoot not to use molasses for it wasn't so good after all.

Source: Thomas W. Polly of Billings, Montana. At the time of this interview, Mr. Polly was seventy-seven years old, had lived in Montana for fifty-eight years, and was one of the local justices of the peace in Billings.
Collector: *Chet M. Simpson*

THE MISADVENTURE OF A TENDERFOOT

A young society man of Malta's early days is the hero of the following story.

His residence in Malta had been very brief, but he had even then been imbued with that primitive masculine instinct: "Give a man a horse he can ride." The Sunday in question was bright and beautiful, a fitting day for knightly adventure. Our hero decided to "go Western" and ventured forth clad in chaps and all the regalia so dear to the heart of a cowboy. He secured a mount from a nearby livery stable and rode gallantly forth. Confident of the correctness of his attire, he was having himself a grand and gorgeous time until some other riders overtook him.

Loud guffaws that would astound a multitude aroused him from his cowboy reveries. Upon closer questioning, his hopes of being regarded as a regular feller vanished as the raindrops in the sun. To his vast dismay he found that the chaps he had so hopefully donned when he ventured forth were on hindside foremost—or in other words fuzzy side down. The story as told in the *Enterprise* closes with the quoted comment, "Perhaps the young gentlemen was under the impression that the fuzzy side of the chaps was to be used as a cushion." The name of the hero rests in oblivion.

Collector: *Gladys W. Miller*

Long-eared Lambs

There was a greenhorn easterner come out to Montana to learn the ways of the West and in time cure his sick lungs. Incidentally he got plenty of lung exercise but I'm getting ahead of my story.

It was during the time of sheep and sheepherders moving into grazing land of Montana's prairies. There were a number of sheep herding jobs open and waiting if you were of a mind to take one. This greenhorn I was speaking of took the notion in his head to want to learn to sheep herd.

"Well," the sheep boss said the first morning to the novice, "there tain't nuthin' to it, son, and 'tis the easiest thing in the world to learn and do. Besides it'll build up your health, too. I want you to be sure to drive all the sheep in this corral at night and be sure to get all the lambs. They're valuable you know. They'll be sheep some day." This particular set-up practiced the corralling of the sheep at night to prevent the coyotes from killing and eating them. The greenhorn promised faithfully that all of this would be carried out in precise order.

The sheep man left the kid on his own for three weeks before he returned to the camp. He came just at sundown and offhand he was pleased because apparently his orders were being carried out right down to a gnat's heel. He noticed the kid seemed to have a healthy flush to his cheeks and an unusual zip to his walk. But the kid looked disgusted.

"How are you doing, son?" asked the sheep boss.

"All right. Fine and dandy except for one thing. Some of those lambs, especially the long-eared ones, give me a lot of trouble. When their ears get long I've never seen it fail. I have to run hell out of them before I can get them in that corral."

"What do you mean long-eared ones?" With that the sheep man looked into the milling and blatting sheep. "Them's not lambs, son, them's jackrabbits."

That was a fact. There were about fifteen of them in that corral with the sheep. No wonder his health improved.

Source: Christopher L. "Chris" Rhinemuth. At the time of this interview, Mr. Rhinemuth was seventy-five years old and a retired railroad man.
Collector: Chet M. Simpson

Snipe Hunting

*O*ne of the diversions of the early-day residents of Big Timber, in south-central Montana, was a game they called snipe hunting. A tenderfoot invariably was invited to go snipe hunting. A long distance from town he would be given a large sack and told to wait while the other members of the party rounded up the snipe. While the tenderfoot waited in the midst of a swamp or by a mosquito-infested creek, the others returned to town. The snipe hunts always took place at night and book agents from the East were the most popular victims of this type of humor.

Source and collector: unknown

Milking a Steer

*I*t was during the days of many steamboats on the Missouri, and competition between the many transportation companies was so keen that every inducement was offered to secure passengers for the trip down the river. One particularly wide-awake captain went so far as to promise fresh milk for their breakfast food and fresh cream for their coffee, although he had not made any arrangements for providing the same. At last his cargo was loaded aboard and with a large passenger list, all congratulating themselves on a trip with plenty of milk and cream for breakfast ahead of them, he weighed anchor and steamed away down toward St. Louis.

It was still the first afternoon, with no breakfasts having occurred yet to mar his serenity, that the captain was leaning over the port rail lazily scanning the passing landscape, when something reminded him that he had a promise to keep to his passengers. The thing that reminded him was the sight of a horned bovine animal contentedly chewing its cud while it basked in the shade of a tree near the bank of the river.

Now the captain being only a riverboat sailor and not a dairy expert wasn't the least bit particular whether his milk supply came from a Holstein or a Jersey, so it made little difference to him that the animal in question was one of that skinny-looking breed called longhorns. He ordered the helm hard aport and called for a couple of seamen, or rather river men, to bring ropes to the gangway. The craft swung to a stop alongside the bank and a gangplank shoved ashore near to where the interested bovine was still chewing its cud and watching operations with a speculative eye. Taking one of the ropes the captain made a loop of it and whirled it over his head in approved cowboy style. Long years of tossing lines to dock posts made him the equal of the average cowboy in tossing a rope, and so the loop settled neatly down over the animal's horns. That animal snorted its distrust and started for the tall timber but the quick footwork of the captain saved the day as he took a turn around a nearby cleat and called for the deckhands to come haul the animal aboard. With many dismayed bellows the critter was forced to walk to the gangway up which she was literally dragged till, his bovine quarry within reach, the captain bethought himself of a place to stable his dairy. He was however relieved of further speculation on the subject for the moment by a wild bellow of righteous anger as the cow aimed her horns for his midriff and charged him in high gear.

The captain nimbly sprang for the top of a cabin safely out of danger, whereupon the cow turned her attention to clearing the decks of the river men who were in sight. She then paraded up and down the main deck inviting anybody to come down and try to MILK HER. Things remained at this stage of development for several moments, and the captain was beginning to wonder how he would manage to run his boat with this ferocious beast pacing the fo'c's'le, when a cowboy came up on deck and surveyed the scene with appreciative gaze.

"What's gong on here?" he asked.

The captain explained, "I promised my passengers fresh milk this trip and so I brought this cow aboard to milk her on the way to Saint Louie."

"Well, of course, if you want the cow on board why that's up to you," the cowboy replied, "but if you expect to get milk from that animal why reckon you're bound to be disappointed pretty quick, because that ain't no cow, that's a steer."

Whereupon the captain blushed and ordered the deckhands to drive the critter back down the gangway. The passengers went without their fresh cream and milk on that trip also!

Collector: Elmer Baird of Roundup, Montana

Horse Trading

*B*ig Gus Thompson of Hardin was a horse trader pure but not simple. His knowledge of animals and his skill at trading was such that he became a nationally prominent figure.

One day Gus was sitting on the porch of the Irma Hotel at Cody, Wyoming in the heart of the dude ranch country. In between greetings from friends he interested himself by picking out the dudes from the natives, looking the horses over and counting the out-of-state automobile licenses. As he sat there a well-dressed dude came up and introduced himself.

"Mr. Thompson," said the dude, "I've heard you're one of the best judges of horse flesh in this part of the country. That you're a man who really knows horses and your judgment is to be trusted."

"Well, that's mighty nice of you, mister." Thompson answered. "That's a mighty nice compliment. What can I do for you?"

"I'd like a horse. A gentle horse that I can trust with my daughter, but I want a good one and a fast one because she knows a little about riding and can take care of herself."

Thompson's ears perked up and he called his son, Ted, meanwhile telling the dude, "I've got just the horse you want. It's a mighty fine animal and fills your requirements—gentle but fast." He turned to his son. "Bring out that sprint horse I got the other day."

The horse was a beauty. Ted had been feeding it raw eggs mixed with its grain and had polished up its coat until it glistened in the rays of the afternoon sun. The horse was gentle but spirited and pranced proudly up and down in front of the dude on the hotel steps.

"That's just the horse I want," declared the dude.

"Well," said Thompson, "he is a beauty and a mighty fine horse, but you shouldn't buy a horse right off the bat like that. I don't want to sell him until you see what he can do. Ted, saddle 'im up."

In a few minutes Ted Thompson was back again with the horse saddled and bridled. He raced the animal up and down the main street of Cody and the horse fairly flew. The dude reached for his wallet and pulled out $200. "I'll take him right now," he insisted. Thompson pocketed the money and went back to counting automobile licenses.

A few days later Thompson was again in his favorite seat on the porch of the Irma Hotel and again the dude appeared before him.

"Mr. Thompson," he sternly asked, "do you remember that horse I bought from you a few days ago?"

"You bet I do," drawled Thompson. "A mighty fine animal. A mighty fine animal."

The dude was not to be denied. "Mr. Thompson," he continued, "did you know that horse was twenty-three years old?"

"Why, yes," answered Thompson. "I do remember something about that."

"And, Mr. Thompson," the dude continued with more of an edge to his voice, "did you know that horse was totally blind in one eye and can barely see out of the other?"

"Why, yes," Thompson confessed, "I did know about that."

The dude transfixed Thompson with a stern, hard glare. "Then, why," he asked coldly, "didn't you tell me about those things?"

Thompson leaned forward confidentially in his chair. His voice still had the same soft, silky drawl. "You see, Mister," he confided, "I bought that horse a short time ago from Bear Paw, down on the Crow Reservation. Bear Paw didn't tell me anything about that and so naturally I thought it was a secret."

Source: E. J. Keeley. Mr. Keeley was a former rider who was, at the time of this interview, a WPA Administration Officer in Butte, Montana.
Collector: Ed Reynolds

PROSPECTORS' PLAY

A prospector with a sluice box.

Photo by K. D. Swan (#373)

THE TALKING MULE

*O*ne of the amusing tales told among the Irish miners at Butte is about a ventriloquist who worked in the Butte mines in the early days. As the story goes, one day the ventriloquist concealed himself behind a pile of mine timbers on a dump near the shaft. A typical "old country" Irishman was driving a mule and timber truck on the dump. As the Irishman and the mule passed near the pile of timbers, the ventriloquist threw his voice and the mule turned and appeared to say, "Please don't beat me." The Irishman checked the mule and gazed in astonishment at the animal. Again from the mouth of the animal appeared to come the appeal of "Please, don't beat me." The Irishman dropped the reins and in a flash dashed down the steep slope of the dump and on down the road. According to the tale, this Irishman was never again seen in Butte.

Source and collector: unknown

LOST TOOTH RAVINE

*S*outh of Cleveland is a deep rock-walled canyon which is called "Lost Tooth Ravine." In this gulch many years ago an old prospector named Jake Plunkett pitched his tent. He had a hunch that gold was to be found there and his hours of arduous toil were limited only by the first streak of dawn and the last glimmer of twilight. His labor proved unsuccessful over a long period, however, and Jake was beginning to doubt the value of the gulch, when a most unfortunate thing happened to him. Panting from his exertions with pick and shovel, he lost his false teeth in the prospect. Mr. Plunkett's diet consisted chiefly of crisply baked bannock and tough sinewy bacon. This menu held forth little chance for a man without any teeth. So, forgetting all about gold, and concentrating all his efforts in the search for the lost denture, Jake worked harder than ever. He worked over all the loose dirt at the bottom of the prospect hole and even went to the trouble of screening it. The elusive plate refused to show up, and the hungry old man was rapidly losing weight because of his inability to chew his rations. Cowboys occasionally rode through the diggings, and they always paused to sneer at Mr. Plunkett and ask if he had found any gold yet.

"Ain't any showed up yet, but I'll find it," was his invariable reply. Finally the old fellow's search was rewarded. The soiled but still useful plate of false teeth came to light in the excavated dirt, and Mr. Plunkett resumed his copious dining on bannock and bacon. So elated was he over his good luck that he could not suppress his desire to make known his find to others. So, mounting his packhorse, he rode into Cleveland. The little post office was filled with cowhands and sheep ranchers when he burst in on them, his seamed and wrinkled old face bathed in a glow of supreme happiness. "I've found it, gents, I've found it," he shouted, "and now I'm a-goin' over to old Ma Pallet's and buy me a nice big steak and onions." This Mr. Plunkett did, thoroughly gorging himself through the efficient service of the recently recovered teeth. Upon returning to the post office, he was surprised to note that all the cowhands had left. Only the postmaster was there, and he was in an exceedingly grouchy humour.

"Gol-dang a job like this anyways. A man cain't leave for five minutes. How big a strike yuh figure yuh made, Jake?" he asked.

"Strike?" repeated Mr. Plunkett. "Whatcha mean strike? I ain't made no strike and never said I did. Where's all the cowboys gone?"

"Gone? Why they's goin' hell bent for the gulch you been workin' in. Sure yuh said yuh found it when yuh came bustin' in here a while ago. I heard yuh myself," said the postmaster. "I sure wanted to go along too and stake out a claim," he added, "but I dassent leave a U.S. Post Office without a postmaster."

"Har har har," roared the aged and well-filled Mr. Plunkett. His laughter was genuine. He never did like the cowboys much. They kidded him on his prospecting activities too much. Now, he joyously ruminated, he would do a little kidding himself. He stayed in Cleveland overnight, and it wasn't until noon next day that the cowboys began to drift back from the canyon. They had each staked out a mining claim, and the only ground not staked was the worthless prospect hold in which Mr. Plunkett's teeth had defied discovery for many days. Surprised at seeing the old man in town, the returning cowboys plied him with questions.

"Why ain't you at the claim takin' out the pay dirt, Jake?" asked one inquisitive cattle rancher.

"Beginnin' to think the old canyon ain't goin' to pan out after all," replied the prospector.

"Well, yuh struck good rock didn't yuh?"

"Me? Well, I should say not. You folks think I'd be fool enough to ride in here and tell yuh if I did?"

"Well yuh did say yuh found it. I hear yuh myself when yuh got to town yestiddy."

"Well so I did find it, yuh block-headed jack-ass," retorted Mr. Plunkett. "What's that got tuh do with all you half-baked hombres gallopin' off and litterin' my canyon up with stakes? Cain't a man lose a plate of false teeth and find 'em again without startin' a gold rush?"

Collector: W. H. Campbell of Chinook, Montana, collected this version of the "oft-repeated tale of Jake Plunkett told by all old-timers of the Bear Paw district."

WAGONWHEEL JOHN'S GOLD

*T*wo men arrived near Fort Benton in the autumn after a long peril-ous trip through the wilds of Montana. Those two men were the leaders of the first expedition to explore the Musselshell Valley and now they were camping to rest their two four-mule teams before the last stage of the journey into Fort Benton. John Zimmerman (Wagonwheel John), one of the two men, walked down to the edge of the nearby stream and scooped up a handful of sand while his companion looked on. "What d'ya say we do some prospecting while we rest up?" Wagonwheel suggested. His companion agreed, and together they started a sluice box and a day or two later they began to carry water from the river to wash the gravel which they had put into the box. Wagonwheel stooped down suddenly and held up a small tiny object. "Gold!" he shouted, and fell to wash-ing his gravel with renewed fervor.

But no more gold showed for his efforts and at last after a few minutes work he threw down his bucket with a snort of disgust. "I'll not be workin' myself into no sweat for a bit o' gold no bigger than that!"

The other man looked at Wagonwheel in open-eyed amaze-ment. "Whay, man, what's wrong wit' yuh! You've only tried for ten minutes and already got two dollars worth of gold. What does yuh expect?"

"Well, you can have my share of it for ten dollars," Wagonwheel shrugged. Whereupon the other man eagerly handed him the money and began working on the sluice while Wagonwheel pock-eted the money and went to lay in the shade.

After ten days the other man threw aside his bucket in disgust. "I mighta knowed you'd got all the gold there was," he sniffed.

Wagonwheel laughed. "I shoulda, it was my own tooth."

Collector: Elmer Baird of Roundup, Montana.

SKOOKUM JOE'S DIARY

June 23rd, 1891. Went to Nye. Old Bill Hamilton back from Canada. Drunk today.

October 2nd, 1891. Three horse thieves hung last night near Red Lodge.

May 17th, 1892. Anarchists hung J. E. Wason at Alpine gulch last night. Stole $8.00 from him. Sheriff in Maiden looking up the case. I don't want to tell who done it.

May 18th, 1892. Stop at Rhodes. Give cat some meat from box. Stay all night. Cat dead in morning. So we don't eat anything here. Think anarchists won't try to run out any white man. Clear this morning so I wash my coat. If it gets dry, I will go to Moccasin.

I. D. O'Donnell had staked Skookum Joe to grub, horses, wagon and tools with the understanding that Joe's finds were to be divided equally between them. With the patient optimism of the born prospector, Joe trudged for years over miles of desolate Montana wilderness, digging into hillsides, panning gravel from creek beds, lonely, weary, and persistent.

He was, Mr. O'Donnell says, a striking figure even in those early days of idiosyncrasies. Grim, taciturn, determined, dressed always in corduroys, and leading a packhorse, he tramped from Maiden to Nye and from Nye to Red Lodge. A man to whom wealth could have no meaning, he devoted his life to the search for gold, and he died a poor man on the eve of a big discovery.

Most of his later days were beset by illness. Enlargement of the heart, the doctor told Mr. O'Donnell, but Joe wrote:

August 26th, 1894. Some gold today. Got very tired today. Feel very lonesome. Think the highlode is center of gold leads. Heat is hell. Nearly sick. Got something. Can't tell yet what it is. Weak. Fever. Take coal oil and whiskey. Feel better.

A few days later:

Got a blacktail buck before I got my pants on this morning. Very sick. Used bottle of most bitter truck I ever tasted. Got the mail. Note from 'Bud' O'Donnell.

The last entries in his diary are:
July 17th, 1895. Note from O'Donnell.
July 18th. Get to Billings.

Joe arrived, Mr. O'Donnell says, a very sick man. That last night Joe said,"We've got it at last, Bud, richest thing in Montana. I'll draw a map so you can locate it easy, but not tonight. I'm too tired. Tomorrow I'll draw a map."

Next morning when the landlady went to Skookum Joe's room she found the fire lit, coffee bubbling on the stove, and Joe dead in his chair, dressed to his hat, bending over to tie his shoelaces. And "the richest thing in Montana" remains a secret still, to be rediscovered sometime, possibly, by a prospector as shrewd and patient as was Skookum Joe.

Source: *Taken from an article by Glendolin Damon Wagner*
Collector: *Edna Felthousen*

JIM OLAFSON'S MOTHER LODE

*J*im Olafson came to Bannack in 1866, from where no one knew. He was a large, fierce looking man about fifty years old, and did not associate much with other miners of the town. He lived in his little cabin on Yankee Flat and sometimes disappeared for a month or more with his pack of grub, blankets, pick and gold pan.

One June morning in 1867, the neighbors saw him leave going toward the south with his prospecting outfit. They thought nothing of it at the time but later had cause to remember his going and especially the direction that he took. In about a week Jim was seen to return. His pack was gone but in its place he carried several ore sample sacks, and immediately went up town to the Goodrich hotel. Striding into the saloon and over to a card table he laid his sacks down. Turning, he said in a loud voice, "Boys, my troubles are over. I've struck the mother lode and I've got samples here to prove it. I ain't gonna file no claims though, to give my place away. You could never find it anyway."

The men in the room thinking he was drunk turned away again until he opened his sacks. What they saw then made them gasp and stare in amazement for on the table lay the richest ore any of them had ever seen. A rough assay of the samples estimated them at

$12,000 per ton, and Jim Olafson became the most important fig-
ure of the day. Men could not be too friendly with him, but through
all their flattery Jim remained close mouthed, never dropping a hint
as to the location of the claim. The miners dogged his footsteps;
they listened by his door at night to hear if he talked in his sleep,
and those who had seen him go away before, told of the direction
he had taken and caused a general stampede into the hills. However, none ever found his claim.

Then one night something in Jim Olafson's brain snapped and
he became a raving maniac. During his delirium he told of a vein
of ore so rich the nuggets could be picked out of it with a pocket-
knife. He was sent to an insane asylum where he died some months
later, never telling his secret.

Men have hunted long for the motherlode without success.
Superstitious remarks accompany the retelling of the tale, for did
not Jim Olafson go insane from it? Old prospectors say it will be
found again some day but that its discovery will cause bad luck to
him who finds it and that he also will be cursed with insanity.

Like many communities Dillon suffers from an oversupply of
tales of buried treasure. One that is given the most credence and
has lured many searching parties is the story of buried gold in Price
Canyon. Road agents looted a stage of $40,000 in gold dust, but
were pursued, captured and strung up. It is still believed that they
buried the treasure in the canyon because the gold has never been
recovered.

Collector: Ed Sommers

THE GREEDY LORD
(FOLKLORE OF "JUGO SLAVIA")

*O*nce there was a lord who was very cruel and very rich. He had a large estate and the people who lived on his land did not like him because they had to give him nearly all they got for their crops. They were allowed just enough for a meager living.

He had so much money he didn't know what to do with it but he still wanted more.

Every night before sunset he went for a walk in a beautiful place full of trees. One evening as he was walking he saw a hut on his estate where an old lady lived. He became very angry because someone was living on his land without his permission. He decided to go and tell the woman to get out of there.

When he came to the hut the woman said, "Good evening lord, come in."

Without saying hello, or good evening, the lord said, "Why didn't you tell me you were going to live here as the others did?"

She answered, "Why are you such a sour cat?"

He was angry with rage. So she said, "I know why you are so angry and what you are thinking about. You are thinking how you could get more money and you can't control yourself for that. I know where you could get a lot of gold, oh, so much that you could never carry it in your life because there is so much."

When the lord heard that he stood petrified and stared at her. Then after a few moments the greedy lord said, "Where is it?"

She said, "I'll tell you if you will sit here on the rock and listen very carefully to me." Then she started to tell him, "You go straight to the forest until you come to a lake. Then turn to the left until you come to a black rock, then take a few steps to the right and just walk straight until you come to the cave. There is a big rock on the entrance of the cave. While you are going don't turn your head left or right or look backward, just keep it straight ahead. When you come to the cave say three times: 'Cave hard and rich give me your gold.' Here, I'll give you a magic flower and pin it on your coat, but watch very closely that you do not lose this flower in the cave, or you'll never come back alive. When you say those magic words the cave will open and you go straight ahead and you will come to a brook. Then take a bucket and dip it into the brook and empty the liquid outside of the cave and as soon as the liquid touches the ground it will turn to gold. But be very careful that you do not lose that flower while you are working. You have just one hour's time to be taking gold out of the brook. Remember what I said."

When he came to the place, he was so greedy and selfish that he carried a huge amount of gold out and the hour was almost over, just one second left, and he thought he would go just once more. While he was running his flower fell in the brook and he couldn't reach it. As soon as the flower fell he heard terrifying, deadly noises just like the devils laughing that the cave was shutting. He started to run thinking he was going to get out yet, but the cave was already shut. The lord cried for help and said he would break the door down but he couldn't. So he was left there buried forever in the cave of gold. Next morning when the workers went to work they saw the gold that the lord had carried out the day before. They were surprised because they never saw it before and didn't know where it came from. Then they went to town and told the people what they had found. All of the people came but they couldn't take the lord's gold. It just stood there. They asked each other, "Where is the lord? We haven't seen him this morning."

No one knew that he went to the cave except the old woman. When she heard the news she just nodded her head and said, "He always was greedy for gold, and the gold buried him and his grave."

Source: Mary Kombol of Roundup, Montana, told this as folklore of Yugoslavia.
Collector: Evelyn M. Rhoden

KELLEY'S LOST MINE

A Great Falls man, who was known to drink too much, was urged by his friends, for his own good, to accompany them on a deer hunt. The company made camp in the northern part of Fergus County. The man in question refused to take part in the deer hunting; having just recovered from a "party," he preferred to wander around the hills himself. He picked up some specimens of Agates and what he considered fool's gold.

After returning to Great Falls he showed his specimens to a dentist in Great Falls and the ones which he called fool's gold were assayed and proved to be very valuable pure gold. He returned to the hills but searched in vain for the mine. He made his home with Charley Kelley while searching and when later he was killed in a train wreck, the lost mine was left to Kelley and it still remains a lost mine.

Collector: Ruth Lewis

AMONG THE MYSTERY MINES

T he early mining business was quite a spicy game, every one for himself. A gentleman once found some float ore on the lower end of a stream near his ranch. On his way to the western coast he left it at Helena to be assayed. It proved to be very valuable, and when he was asked where he found it, he airily replied: "In the West."

As he resided in the Judith Mountains, the assayer suspected the ore was from there and had him watched for the purpose of finding the mine. But this gentleman had no more idea where it was than his rivals and neither of them ever located it. So it still remains among the Mystery Mines.

Collector: Ruth Lewis

MOTHER NATURE'S WINTER WRATH

Adventurers inspecting a
crevasse on Sperry Glacier,
Glacier National Park.

Photo by R. E. Marble (#237)

MOTHER NATURE'S
WINTER WRATH

ICE EYES

That winter of '98–'99 was the damnedest, coldest winter I ever saw in Montana and one of the strangest things happened to my horses.

I had a ranch on Poverty Flats near Joliet, Montana and the snow and blizzardy weather had driven every rancher into his cabin. Nobody ventured out very far until it became an absolute necessity to get some coal. A number of the fellers got their grain boxes on sleds and went to town to get some coal. Everybody was bundled up to the eyes with all the clothes they ever had to their name. Every once in a while in driving to town you had to get out and walk alongside of your sled-wagon to keep warm. It was a terrible cold.

We got into town and there must have been seven or eight ranchers there with a sled-wagon waiting for the coal train to come down from Red Lodge. When the coal train did arrive, the engineer said he didn't have any coal to leave there. He said he didn't have orders to leave any. I told him that I had a wife and baby that was almost freezing to death and I had to have some coal. The rest of the ranchers were bunched up around the engineer and they all had blood in their eye and he could see it.

He made a pretty good feller of hisself by saying, "Well, if you fellers want any coal, go ahead and help yourself but I ain't supposed to be looking. And don't take too much off of any one car." We sure pitched into that coal train and got as much as we figured we could get home with safely.

I only had three and a half miles to get home but you know it took me almost ten hours to get there. I couldn't figure out what kept those two horses a-goin' in spite of all the handicaps. Some places the snow was drifted so high that I had to stop and break through the drift myself so the horses would know where to go. Sometimes the horses' heads were on a level with the sled wagon loaded with coal—the snowdrifts were that high.

When about a mile away from my place, I thought I couldn't make it. I mustered up a lot of courage to go that remaining mile. If it wasn't for the good old steady plugging of those horses, I don't think I would have tried it. I had icicles on my eyelids and two or three icicles that were a good three inches long a hangin' on my nose. I was so cold I didn't bother to knock them off. I didn't know it at the time but I had frozen my ears and forehead and the skin peeled off for days afterwards.

I finally got to the ranch house and I found when putting my horses in the barn that the horses had big balls of ice frozen over each of their eyes. I got my wife to help me and we warmed up these balls of ice by our hands and by blowing our breath on them to get them to come off the horses. At that all the horses' eye lashes came out along with the ball of ice.

I was warmed up pretty well then because I'd been in the house by a pretty darned hot fire from the new coal I'd gotten and just had a good hot supper in my guts. I got the crazy idea of putting one of those ice eyes over my own and see what I could see. I thought I could get a horse's eye view of things. Sure enough when I looked through one of those balls of ice that had been over a horse's eye, I saw the damnedest sight. You could see nothing but fields of clover and pan after pan of oats and haystacks until hell wouldn't have it. No wonder those horses kept going and going when they saw such things as that.

Source: E. L. "Dick" Grewell of Billings, Montana. At the time of this interview, Mr. Grewell was seventy-one years old, a retired rancher, and had lived in Montana for fifty-two years.
Collector: Chet M. Simpson

IN SEARCH OF OLD BALDY

I *remember about the coldest sub-zero weather in my life and I nearly lost my life incidentally.* It was the winter of 1904 or 1905.

We, the cowhands and I, had got the little over two thousand head in the draws and coulees where they were protected from the direct wind. It had snowed and snowed for about two days steady. Then it suddenly quit and the temperature dropped fast. The box elder and cottonwood trees along the creek snapped and crackled as I and the boys rode our broncs back to the ranch house.

One of the boys says to me casual-like, "That north wind is comin' up fast, Boss. By the way, whar wuz Old Baldy today? I don't remember seeing him in the herd." Old Baldy was a white-faced Hereford steer I'd kept for years. He was a lead steer and I'd never sold him, but he was as temperamental as a woman. Sometimes when the herd refused to follow him, he would pull a pout and stay for days off in the hills just to have his way. It struck me immediately that was what happened early this morning. "Well," I says to the cowhand, "I'd better go round him up."

The rest of the boys wanted to go themselves. No. I wouldn't have it. I told them to take care of my horse and I would go a foot. The snow was about shin deep. I got my overshoes and started out. I had in mind the north draw. Baldy often peeved in that ravine. What fooled me was the sky. It was clear and the sun was shining but it didn't mean anything. Somebody had completely turned off the heat.

A brisk wind was coming up from the north and it felt like it had kissed the north pole at least twice. By the time I had reached the middle of the draw I found myself stopping often to stomp my feet and slap my hands and arms against my sides to keep circulation going and to keep warm.

I heard a slapping, thrashing noise behind me and looked around to see what it was. The sight surprised me. Here was my shadow stomping its feet and beating its arms against its sides and I wasn't moving a finger. Boy! I realized it surely was cold.

I called out "Baldy! Baldy!" a couple of times. No answer and I couldn't see any trace of him. My face and forehead began to feel numb. I realized I must be freezing to death. I was dressed extremely warm too. Heavy red flannels, two pairs of pants, three coats, a big sheepskin coat, a heavy fur-lined cap, and fur-lined mittens. But I was freezing.

I sleepily realized I must get back to the ranch. I turned around to go but I found I couldn't move an inch. Something was tugging at my coat and pants. Turning my head around I saw what was causing all the standstill. My shadow was frozen to the surface of the snow. It had one hand free, however, and was beckoning me to come and help it to free itself.

Immediately I recognized the emergency and rushed to its aid.

All I had was a Bowie knife. I extracted it from my pocket and cut my shadow free from the snow surface. But I was much exhausted and fell to the ground in a frozen stupor. My shadow was so grateful for what I had done for it and wanting to repay my kindness, it picked me up and threw me over its shoulder. Then it proceeded to carry me back to the ranch house where the hands helped thaw me out. I wouldn't be alive this very day. The boys will swear to it. Course some of 'em are dead and others scattered all over tarnation.

Source: Ralph L. Simpson of Billings, Montana. At the time of this interview, Mr. Simpson was sixty-five years old and a retired rancher. His ranch was located on Cold Creek of Shane Ridge between what are now known as Columbus and Joliet, Montana.
Collector: Chet M. Simpson

FROZEN SOLID

*M*r. O'Donnell is a human tome of Montana history and with especial emphasis on the Yellowstone Valley. When asked for a "tall tale" from his fund of western experiences, he replied as follows:

I know one or two. This story was told to me by "Teddy" Blue. Blue was walking across some of the range he owned when a blizzard came up suddenly. The cold penetrated his heavy clothing with apparent ease. He looked around for some shelter or cabin where he could get warm. He spied down in a coulee a man squatting near a fire and warming his hands. Blue walked toward the joyous sight of the fire in anticipation of warming himself. As he arrived at the fire he thought he'd give the stranger a playful kick.

"Howdy Pardner," he said, but he retrieved his foot in a hurry for the man was froze as solid as a rock.

He thought then that he would warm himself anyway. His disappointment was only aggravated greater for he found that the flames of the fire were frozen solid.

Source: Ignatius D. "Bud" O'Donnell of Billings, Montana. At the time of this interview, Mr. O'Donnell was eighty-one years old and had spent sixty years in Montana.
Collector: Chet M. Simpson

Shooting Frozen Wolves

T his story pertains to the severe winter of 1886–1887, which caused the stockmen all over the country heavy losses of cattle, horses and sheep. This story was told to me by Edward Silverthorne and sworn to by him as being true, although several whom I asked said that he probably invented the story, although it was cold enough to freeze anything.

I will try and put it on paper, as nearly as possible, the way it was told to me. I quote:

When me and my uncle, Benjamin Reid, came to Fergus County in 1882, I didn't start right in raising cattle. I was just a young feller and being a good rider and all, I had no trouble in getting jobs as a range rider. I had several jobs, and all of them with pretty large outfits. My first job was workin' for T. C. Power, owner of the Horseshoe Bar spread. I worked for Power from 1882 to 1885 and made quite a little money, which I hoped to buy cattle with when I finally settled down. After I quit Power, I took a job with the N-Bar Ranch, owned by Tommy Cruse. I liked Tommy fine. He was a good boss and paid good wages to his hands. He like me too and in the spring he asked me if I would like to go to Idaho and bring back a herd of cattle for him and his partner, Charles Aneeney. Well, being a young feller and restless-like, I jumped at the chance to go.

So in the spring of 1886, me and two other men and Tommy started out for the Lemhi Valley in Idaho to get a herd of 2,500 head of shorthorns, mostly two-year-old heifers. We had a fine time and got the cattle and started herding them back to Montana. All along the trail, Tommy would buy horses and trail them along with the cattle. I reckon it was about September when we got to where we was to range the cattle, a place known as the Bull Mountains. All went along just as good as you please until one morning, we misses some of the horses which we bought and figured they had went back to their old stamping grounds. It was mighty cold that morning and the temperature went away down to about twenty-five below zero. It was just my luck to be picked, along with Johnny Gamble, to go out in search of the missing horses. Well, we started out, bright and early, that September morning and I guess we rode all over hell, looking for them strays. We asked several ranchers along the trail if they had seen any stray horses and they said no, so on we went. I guess we were too cold to reason good but finally we got to Sixteenmile Creek and ran smack into one of the worst blizzards in the whole history of Montana. We got so dadblamed cold that we quit the search for those damn horses right now and begun to look for shelter of some kind. The wind was blowing the snow so hard you couldn't see in front of you and our eyes froze icicles.

Finally we come across Peck Williams' place and went in to git warm. We suffered misery until we thawed out our bones which was about six hours. In that time, the snow had piled up considerable so you couldn't see out the windows and the door was banked shut. Peck had a thermometer outside his window and we noticed that it dropped to almost sixty below zero. The worst part of it was we had to stay cooped up in that house for about forty days and nights while the wind howled and the snow blew. It is the hardest thing in the world for two men to have to stick sit out together for that length of time without going complete loco, let alone three of us. We did almost go crazy with nothing to do but sit and eat and sleep.

Well, it was about December when the blizzard let up somewhat and me and Johnny decided to leave. We hadn't got far when we noticed the carcasses of frozen cattle and horses lying all over the ground. Why, you could walk for a mile or two in any direction and never have to step off of a carcass. Well, we never did find those horses and decided that they had run off with the storm or froze to death somewhere. We decided to head back for the Bull Mountains and see how Tommy and the other boys were making out. We had just reached camp when another awful one of those blizzards started in. What cattle were left begun to freeze on account of not having enough to eat and were weak from the other blizzard. There was a lot of trees around our camp and the wolves and coyotes would put up an awful howl which lasted through the night. One night, the bunch of us decided to put a stop to the wolves and coyotes, which kept us awake at night. We were jumpy as newborn colts anyhow and those wolves was the last straw. We could see them from our camp, standing around in a bunch, their eyes glowing in the dark. They were only about 150 yards from us and right in plain sight. Well, I was considered a good shot with a rifle in those days so I thought I would git myself some of those wolves.

One evening, before it got dark, I took my rifle and resting it on a fork of a pine tree, I took several shots at a bunch of the critters. They were all standing up in a group and made easy targets, but after shooting about five bullets and not seeing any of the wolves fall, I blamed it on my gun when the other boys started ribbing me.

I told them to take a shot and see if they could do any better. Each one of them shot but the same thing happened. The wolves just didn't fall.

The next morning, the temperature was below sixty degrees. We started out to see why we hadn't killed any of the coyotes, walking very easy with our guns ready to shoot if they made a move. We knew they were gaunt and hungry and would maybe try and charge us but when we got up close, we all got a good laugh. They were dead as doornails but our bullets hadn't killed them, no, they were plumb frozen to death. We found where every one of our bullets had made a hit but the wolves were frozen before we shot at them. We counted eight holes in one wolf and you could see plumb through him. He was frozen that hard, that the bullet just left a round hole all the way through him. You could see daylight on the other side of several of the animals. Those same wolves had eaten several of our young calves because we found their bones plumb clean of any meat.

Well, that is the worst winter I ever put in in Montana and since that time the weather has seemed very mild with the exception of 1894 when it got very cold but not as cold as in 1886–1887. Do you know how many head of cattle we had left of the 2,500 head the next spring? We had about 125 head left, and some of them died because they were too weak to pull through after that cold spell. We don't know how many those wolves got before they froze to death, but they got enough as we could see by the bones laying around. We sure helped them to keep fat that winter. I don't know if you will believe this story or not, but it is true. Lots of people don't believe it and I can't prove nothing. I know it's true because I was there when it happened. End of quote.

Source: William Buchanan, Jr.

PACK RAT DUMPLINGS

*S*omehow *I got stranded in a line cabin one blizzardy winter. I* couldn't get out and nobody could get to me. Those Montana winters would put to shame any severe winter we have nowadays and these "rough" ones now would seem like a snow squall compared to them North Pole specials we had.

Day after day about all I had to do was keep the fire up in the pot-bellied stove and cook myself some grub. The wind howled and howled outside and the coyotes and wolves howled with it at night. It was scary and at nights I'd go to bunk with all the artillery I had in my possession which was two six-shooters and a rifle along with plenty of ammunition. That cabin musta been located on a nest of pack rats fer they practically took over the place. They was after what little grub I had left which was about a half a sack of flour. I had to put a rope on the sack of flour and hoist it nearly half way up to a rafter. Then the rascals would climb up to and on the rafter and try to scale down to the flour. I fixed this a little by hangin' the sack over the hot stove so that when they fell they's generally hit the hot stove and put a brand on 'em before they could skiddoo.

Well, these pesky pack rats led me a miserable life. They stole all my socks and left grass straws fer swap and they gnawed my pants belt in several places; maybe fer the salty sweat there. I killed with my six-shooter a number of 'em while they's pokin' their heads out of a hole. It was hell livin' alone like that with that wind howlin' bloody murder and them rats scurryin' around the cabin and almost in the notion of gnawin' a leg offen your carcass. I nearly went nuts and I was talkin' to myself most of the day and night. I was hollerin' at the top of my voice, "Come on out you blankety-blank rats and fight like a man"; and I was standin' in the middle of the floor with both guns drawed. My nerves were rubbed raw.

I was not only goin' battier than a crazy loon but I was starvin' to death. If I just had some meat to cook with that flour it wouldn't be so bad. Why not cook up them rats. I'd been shootin' 'em back in to their holes. I rigged up a rawhide snare and with a sprinklin' of flour in front of a hole it worked like a top. I got five of the rascals in less time than it takes to wink your eye. They fought like tigers and bit hell out of the rawhide thong before I caved in their skulls with a pine knot.

I never came nearer being a cannibal in my life. After degutting 'em and makin' dumplings out of 'em, it sure hit that vacant spot in my belly. It sounds crazy but them pack rat dumplings shore tasted good. A few days later some of the boys got to my cabin and rescued me.

Source: William E. "Billy" Huntington of Lockwood, Montana. At the time of this interview, Mr. Huntington was seventy-nine years old and had spent sixty-five years in Montana.
Collector: Chet M. Simpson

RIDIN' A SHADOW

*M*ontana used to have some terrible cold winters. I know one time that I got lost huntin' for some stock along Rock Creek. It was a nice sunshiny winter day in the morning when I started out. It looked like it might do some meltin'. Suddenly the wind changed into the north and a blast of that wind straight into your face would about freeze your nose off. I was dressed pretty warm but I might as well have been out in that blizzard in the nude for all the good the clothes done me. That wind cut through your clothes like a knife.

I walked and walked and I couldn't find those lost stock. I could hear the creek water freezing solidly to the bottom of the creek. You could hear constant snap and boom noise. I knew I must get home but that sun a-shinin' and the sky so clear like that sure fooled me. The sun might as well have been a picture hung in the sky for all the heat that it gave off.

I saw a black-tailed deer standing off near the direction in which I had to go to get home. So I walked over there thinking I might ride the deer home because I'd heard it could be done. I came up alongside of the deer and it still stood there dumb-like as though it were hypnotized. I touched its eye lid and it never batted an eye lash, and it was colder than a frozen tombstone. Seeing is believin' but I could hardly believe my own eyes. A deer frozen solid right in its own tracks.

I started away and then I noticed a peculiar thing. The deer's shadow was trottin' and gambolin' around me playful-like. Looking over at the frozen deer I could see it had no shadow. This deer-shadow nudged me with its nose and was trying to tell me something. Immediately I got the idea through my cold skull. It wanted me to get on its back for a ride.

I leaped on its back and grabbed a hold of its horns and away we went. I could not realize how this was possible. Here I was skimmin' through the air sittin' down. The deer-shadow seemed to know where I lived for it headed straight to my house. We were goin' at a high rate of speed, much faster than a good racehorse could go. I could hear the soft tappity-tap of the deer-shadow's feet as it raced along on the frozen snow.

Suddenly a live doe leaped out in front of me and we swerved toward it. The deer-shadow was a stag and couldn't resist the charms of a strange doe. It tore out after that doe and I began to beat it with my hand across the rump. I might as well have been fannin' my britches for all the good it seemed to be doin'.

Theoretically it was all good and proper but actually I was hittin' nuthin'.

Surprised as I was at everything, I was to be more surprised for the deer-shadow switched sharply and headed for my house again at break-neck speed. I didn't know how to stop him and when about a hundred yards from my cabin, I was yellin' whoa at the top of my lungs.

The deer-shadow went right through the log cabin and left me plastered up against the side for a minute until I fell to the ground in one big, frozen lump.

Just then one of the fellers in the bunkhouse hit me smack on the head with their boot and I woke up. "Say," this guy says, "what in tarnation is the matter with you, Dick? Musta bin bad dreamin' because you shore was hollerin' whoa to stop some run-away nags."

Source: E. L. "Dick" Grewell of Billings, Montana. At the time of this interview, Dick was seventy-one years old, a retired rancher, and had lived in Montana for fifty-two years.
Collector: Chet M. Simpson

PRACTICES, REMEDIES, AND GENERALLY ACCEPTED LORE

The Buffalo Hunter

Illustrated by W. J. Mead in 1937 for

the Montana Writers' Project tale

"The Cure for the Greedy Hunter."

THE CURE FOR A GREEDY HUNTER

Those hunters who go into the woods each year with a burning desire to slaughter any animal that comes within range of their rifle and who do not abide by the sportsman's rule as to "bag limit," might well take a lesson from the fate that befell one Paul Siskyou, an intrepid but greedy hunter, who roamed the plains back in the early eighties.

Paul Siskyou made a business of buffalo hunting. He chose a spot somewhere in the area that today comprises Hill and Blaine Counties, and making sure that no Indian hunters were in the neighborhood at the time, he slaughtered buffalo by the score. Other white hunters, as well as the Indians, objected to this wanton killing, as they knew that Siskyou could not profit from such large killings. Time and again other hunters arrived at one of his stands shortly after he had pulled out, and to their consternation they found many carcasses lying about which had never been skinned. The more intelligent white men knew that in time the buffalo would become extinct, and they firmly believed that no hunter should kill more of the animals than he could use in the ordinary channels of the trade.

Siskyou was a stubborn, unsociable man, and when other whites attempted to point out to him the needless waste he was incurring in his unlimited buffalo killings, he laughed in their faces and told them that the only reason they were sore was that they were not capable of bringing the animals down with such unerring aim as he daily showed in his hunting activities. According to legend, the Cree Indians who made frequent hunting expeditions into the area, decided on taking more drastic means of making Mr. Siskyou cut down on his bag. They silently rode up on him in the early dawn of a clear bright day. He was located in a stand, which offered him ideal facilities for cutting down a large buffalo herd. His old and reliable 30-30 was trained on the center of the herd, and the grazing monarchs of the prairie were about to be decimated, when strong Cree arms encircled Mr. Siskyou's waist, and he was lifted to the back of an Indian cayuse. His feet tied by strong buckskin thongs beneath the belly of the horse, Mr. Siskyou was forced to accompany his captors, and in a few hours found himself the sole occupant of a teepee, in the midst of a Cree encampment across the Canadian border. It was not the intention of his captors to put him through any physical torture. An old chief of the tribe had thought of a more effective way to make the greedy hunter hate the sight of buffalo. For many days he was kept in the teepee, and three times each day food was brought to him. The menu was unvaried, however, and it consisted solely of buffalo steak, broiled rare over the campfires of the Indians. Spring water was the only other item included on the bill-of-fare. Salt and pepper were not used in seasoning the meat. When three weeks had elapsed, Mr. Siskyou had become so tired of buffalo meat that he loathed the name. He refused to eat any more steaks, and this may have been more the result of stomach revulsion than pure cussedness on his part. Arraigned before the chief of the tribe, Siskyou was willing to promise that never again would he indulge in wild orgies of buffalo killing. He agreed to limit his pelts to the number recognized as reasonable by other hunters, and, having satisfied his captors that he was sincere, they furnished him a pinto horse and set him free.

Siskyou's later years were spent in the army, and he proved himself a soldier of sterling qualities. When he had finally been pensioned and was living in an old soldier's home, some well-meaning residents of the town decided to give the old fellow a treat at Christmastime. A domesticated herd of buffalo was being reduced at the time, and buffalo meat was on the market in that locality during the festive season. On Christmas Day the old campaigners were seated around the large dining table, and Mr. Siskyou's mouth was watering at the thought of the succulent roasted turkey which would soon be brought in. Instead a large platter of fried buffalo steaks was placed on the table, and the retired soldiers entered into the repast with great zest, as it had been many years since they had enjoyed such a treat. Not for Mr. Siskyou did the happy Christmas dinner prove a treat however. Sniffing the odor of buffalo meat, and casting a disgusted glance at the platter he made a hasty exit from the room, and waddled on his stiff old legs as fast as he could to a nearby restaurant, where roast turkey headed the day's menu sheet.

Whether the above happenings actually entered into Paul Siskyou's western career is beside the point. It is a fact that the legend is still used in persuading young hunters who slay beyond the bag limit to curtail their greedy desires when in the woods.

Source: William Harmon of Chinnok, Montana. Mr. Harmon was a veteran soldier and scout who saw active service in the United States Army during the early Indian campaigns in Montana.
Collector: W. H. Campbell of Chinook, Montana

Horse Charmer's Secret

*M*any *ranchmen at some time or other have witnessed and marveled over the seemingly miraculous powers possessed and exerted by that more or less mysterious character of the range land, the horse charmer.*

And more than often, miraculous indeed seemed the work of this gentry, who with no other apparent implement but a battered hat in hand, could call and cajole the most vicious and untameable of horses from field or corral. And in a surprisingly short time have the once fractious beast eating from his hand, apparently as gentle as any tame mouse on the ranch.

The horse charmer invariably claimed his uncanny power over the horse due to his own personal magnetism or a sort of hypnotism that he was able to exert over the animal. Some claim to have inherited the power, claiming it to have been passed on from father to son. Many traveling band of gypsies possessed this magic and it was not an uncommon sight to see an entire band of horses following one lone gypsy, a sort of pied piper arrangement.

But now at last the secret is out. Some horse charmer talked, perhaps in his cups, but talk he did nevertheless; and the priceless secret of his trade is now common property of many ranch hands.

The secret is not hypnotism, mesmerism, sixth sight or any personal charm. The answer is found in that common old root, dug up in many of our grandmothers' gardens.

Asafetida is the solution of the whole pocus-pocus.

Yes, that same smelly herb that in the nineties was placed in a bag by doting mothers and hung around the neck of their innocent offspring to ward off contagious diseases.

Horses love it.

There is a certain property or active agent contained in the herb that acts on a horse as does catnip to a cat. Carrots possess this same property to a small degree, hence the horse's love for that succulent vegetable.

Once the horse charmer learned the secret of the animal's love for the asafetida root, his procedure was simple. An ample quantity of the herb was obtained and reduced to a powder. This was thoroughly rubbed and permeated into all of the charmer's clothes. Special attention was given to his hat and its sweatband. This part of his apparel literally reeked of the offensive asafetida.

When ready for his performance, the charmer would merely place himself in a position where the penetrating odor would reach the horse's nostrils. A horse could smell it for over a mile. The animal's deep-born instinct did the rest. An adequate term fits in here. The horse is claimed by scientists to be allergic to asafetida. He cannot resist it and, all the remainder of the horse charmer's act is so much bunkum and merely for effect. It is the asafetida that the animal desires and the more of the herb rubbed into the charmer's person, the greater his ability as a horse charmer.

The nauseating smell of the root emitting from the charmer's person was generally concealed from humans by the otherwise horsey odor with which the charmer surrounded himself. The smell of asafetida, added to the smell of horse, was more or less indiscernible to the average ranch hand's olfactory organs.

Source: *Jerome Monaghan*
Collector: *William A. Burke*

REPTILIAN BEDFELLOW

*M*en sleeping in the open on the ground have often had the *unpleasant experience of waking up in the morning to find a* *rattlesnake coiled cosily up on their chest or in amongst their blankets.* Obviously the snake means only to imbibe warmth from his erstwhile enemy, but the predicament is none too soothing to the man who realizes that his slightest move may cause the snake to strike and perhaps bury his deadly fangs in the man's chest, face, or some other part of the body. Many years of observation finally led to the conclusion among ranchmen and cowboys that a rattlesnake will very seldom strike a horse on the lower part of the horse's leg, but that horses bit by rattlesnakes were most always struck on the stomach or on the nose, both places where the hair is very short. Whereby it was deduced that rattlesnakes must have a very deep dislike for horsehair, and that the only times they ever struck at horses was when a horse happened to lay down or roll on them, or when a horse should happen to put his nose too close while eating grass. Following out these observations it came to be an accepted fact that men who wished to sleep on the ground in the open could protect themselves from the friendly companionship of a reptilian bedfellow by coiling a horsehair rope around their bed whenever they slept on the open prairie. This fact is probably the only plausible explanation for what little popularity horsehair ropes ever enjoyed among cowboys, as most cowboys seldom ever used a horsehair rope for roping.

Source: Elmer Baird of Roundup, Montana

DOG LORE

*B*lue-eyed or marble-eyed dogs are thought to be the smartest dogs for working stock. Black collies are believed to be better workers than tan or yellow collies. Hairy-faced dogs are believed to be better sheep dogs than open-faced dogs. Police dogs are never trusted with livestock and there seems to be a strong dislike for police dogs

of all description. In the Musselshell Valley many people even go
so far as to dislike the owner of the dog.

Source: Elmer Baird of Roundup, Montana

HORSE LORE

A horse that is hard to break is often considered to be more desirable
after it is broke than a horse that is easy to break. This is because a
very wild horse is thought to have a stronger spirit, which will
cause it to give its last ounce of strength when its master needs it
badly. A very wild horse that has been well broke is usually thought
to be more faithful to its master than an ordinary easily broke horse.
These beliefs all have their foundation on facts of range history.

In estimating the character or value of horses there are a number of traits or tests in judging them. One such method is
concerning the horse's feet and it goes thus: "One white foot look
him over; two white feet try him; three white feet buy him; four
white feet no good." In picking horses for rodeo buckers it is always kept in mind that sleepy or lazy acting horses are generally
the best buckers. Once a horse throws a man it is believed that it
will be twice as hard for the next man to ride him.

A horse is often called "locoed" when it acts jumpy or seems
unusually dumb. A locoed horse is really a horse that has eaten of
the weed called locoweed, which grows in many parts of
Musselshell County. The effects of the loco weed are to make the
horse literally crazy so that it will gallop wildly across the range
running into cliffs, over steep embankments, bumping into trees
or other obstacles until it is completely exhausted or until it kills
or cripples itself by its headlong actions. A locoed horse never

seems to completely regain its senses whether it lives through the first experience or not. It is not known for certain whether there is enough lure in the weed to make the horse want more of it or not.

Source: Elmer Baird of Roundup, Montana

Cures for Snakebites

For rattlesnake bite, kill a chicken and put fresh meat of chicken on the bite.

For snakebite, chop off the head of the snake, pound the head of the snake to pulp with a rock, place smashed head over the snakebite. Or, pound the bones of snake to a powder. Put powder of snake bones on the snakebite.

Russian people put live frogs stomach over the bite of the snake—put a different frog on every ten minutes. May need four or five frogs. The first frog jumps quite a bit, the next one less and less and the fifth one very little.

Source: Mary Kombol of Roundup, Montana found these cures in a "Jugoslavian Doctor Book."
Collector: Evelyn M. Rhoden

Old-time Loggers' Home Remedies

*T*he old time loggers had many home remedies. Here are some of them:

Fat bacon around your neck with dirty woolen sock was good for colds.

Bunkhouses were always closed tight at night because the night air brought many diseases.

Never change your clothes when you get wet. Let them dry on you or you'll catch cold.

Put your underwear on in the fall and leave it on until spring. If you change it you'll catch cold.

Put a chew of tobacco on any wound to prevent infection. This is very good to prevent lockjaw.

Source: Fay G. Clark, Professor of Forest Management, School of Forestry, Montana State University
Collector: Edward B. Reynolds

The TwoDot line features classic western literature and history. Each book celebrates and interprets the vast spaces and rich culture of the American West.

TWODOT
An Imprint of Falcon Publishing

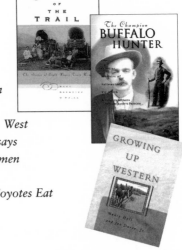

Bozeman and the Gallatin Valley: A History
Charlie's Trail: The Life and Art of C.M. Russell
Flight of the Dove: The Story of Jeannette Rankin
Jeannette Rankin: Bright Star in the Big Sky
Men with Sand: Great Explorers of the American West
Montana Campfire Tales: Fourteen Historical Essays
More Than Petticoats: Remarkable Montana Women
The Only Good Bear is a Dead Bear
Today I Baled Some Hay to Feed the Sheep the Coyotes Eat

It Happened in Series

Entertaining and informative, each book is written in a lively, easy-to-read style, and features 31-34 stories about events that helped shape each state's history.

It Happened in Arizona
It Happened in Colorado
It Happened in Montana
It Happened in New Mexico
It Happened in Oregon
It Happened in Southern California
It Happened in Texas
It Happened in Utah
It Happened in Washington

Four-Legged Legends Series

Young adult readers will be enthralled and inspired by these true tales of animal bravery, loyalty, and ferocity.

Four-Legged Legends of Colorado
Four-Legged Legends of Montana
Four-Legged Legends of Oregon

FALCON®
To order check with your local bookseller or call Falcon at
1-800-582-2665.
Ask for a FREE catalog featuring a complete list of titles on nature, outdoor recreation, travel, and the West.

FALCON GUIDES ® Leading the Way™

FALCON GUIDES ® are available for where-to-go hiking, mountain biking, rock climbing, walking, scenic driving, fishing, rockhounding, paddling, birding, wildlife viewing, and camping. We also have FalconGuides on essential outdoor skills and subjects and field identification. The following titles are currently available, but this list grows every year. For a free catalog with a complete list of titles, call FALCON toll-free at 1-800-582-2665.

BIRDING GUIDES
Birding Minnesota
Birding Montana
Birding Northern California
Birding Texas
Birding Utah

FIELD GUIDES
Bitterroot: Montana State Flower
Canyon Country Wildflowers
Central Rocky Moutnain
  Wildflowers
Great Lakes Berry Book
New England Berry Book
Pacific Northwest Berry Book
Plants of Arizona
Rare Plants of Colorado
Rocky Mountain Berry Book
Scats & Tracks of the
  Pacific Coast States
Scats & Tracks of the Rocky Mtns.
Tallgrass Prairie Wildflowers
Western Trees
Wildflowers of Southwestern Utah
Willow Bark and Rosehips

WALKING
Walking Colorado Springs
Walking Denver
Walking Portland
Walking St. Louis
Walking Virginia Beach

FISHING GUIDES
Fishing Alaska
Fishing the Beartooths
Fishing Florida
Fishing Glacier National Park
Fishing Maine
Fishing Montana
Fishing Wyoming
Fishing Yellowstone Natl. Park

PADDLING GUIDES
Floater's Guide to Colorado
Paddling Minnesota
Paddling Montana
Paddling Okefenoke
Paddling Oregon
Paddling Yellowstone & Grand
  Teton National Parks

ROCKHOUNDING GUIDES
Rockhounding Arizona
Rockhounding California
Rockhounding Colorado
Rockhounding Montana
Rockhounding Nevada
Rockhound's Guide to
  New Mexico
Rockhounding Texas
Rockhounding Utah
Rockhounding Wyoming

HOW-TO GUIDES
Avalanche Aware
Backpacking Tips
Bear Aware
Desert Hiking Tips
Hiking with Dogs
Leave No Trace
Mountain Lion Alert
Reading Weather
Route Finding
Using GPS
Wild Country Companion
Wilderness First Aid
Wilderness Survival

ROCK CLIMBING GUIDES
Rock Climbing Colorado
Rock Climbing Montana
Rock Climbing New Mexico
  & Texas
Rock Climbing Utah
Rock Climbing Washington

■ *To order any of these books, check with your local bookseller or call FALCON ® at **1-800-582-2665**.*
www.FalconOutdoors.com

FALCON®